D1207598

A WORD IN EDGEWAYS

By the same author

IVOR BROWN'S BOOK OF WORDS
I GIVE YOU MY WORD
SAY THE WORD
NO IDLE WORDS
HAVING THE LAST WORD
I BREAK MY WORD

A WORD IN EDGEWAYS

by

IVOR BROWN

JONATHAN CAPE
THIRTY BEDFORD SQUARE
LONDON

FIRST PUBLISHED 1953

PRINTED IN GREAT BRITAIN IN THE CITY OF OXFORD
AT THE ALDEN PRESS
BOUND BY A. W. BAIN & CO. LTD., LONDON

FOREWORD

ONCE more into the breach of promise. I had vowed to end these word-books at Number Six, *Having the Last Word*. I then perjured myself by going on to Number Seven, *I Break my Word*. And here I emerge as an oath-breaker once again. I use a new title kindly supplied by one of my stimulators. It has been my habit to put the responsibility on my correspondents who ply me with fruitful suggestions and with requests compelling me to do some research that leads to more writing. I have repeatedly told them that they are foolish to write my books for me, or rather to employ me as a sub-editor handling their unpaid 'copy' and then to allow me to snatch the rewards of their voluntary services. I can only hope that I am a capable sub-editor and contribute sufficiently in that office. My journalistic experience has taught me that sub-editing, which is the preparation of other people's work by the vigilant correction of mistakes and by the cutting and dressing of the text, is of primary importance to a newspaper and also to a book. If all authors' work were issued to the public in the form in which it reaches the publisher's office and without sub-editorial handling, the plight of the book trade might be considerably worse than it is today. This I put forward as a slight defence of my exploitation of other people's notions, memories and discoveries. At the same time I can bravely and honestly say that my books are partly my own work. A number of the words discussed have indeed been my discovery!

One protest I would like to make. I am often appealed to as an Authority on Words. I am nothing of the kind. I have never been anything so solemn as a Professor of Semantics or an Etymological Expert. I delve in dictionaries, but I never contribute to them. I would not dare. Nor can I lay down the laws on Usage. The Authorities are there, and to them I dedicate this little book, conscious of the amount I owe to them, to Eric Partridge for his verbal omniscience and his global – can I use that word without rebuke? – range of information, to Mr. V. H. Collins and to Mr. G. H. Vallins for their wisdom in the choice and grouping of words and, of course, to Sir Ernest Gowers, the linguistic counsellor of the Civil Service. At intervals Sir Alan Herbert, who was one of the first to prick commercial and bureaucratic heavy-handedness in the use of words, returns to the battle-field, a man always welcome in any side which he joins.

My only excuse for writing is affection for words, and affection is not the same as knowledge. A lover of woman is not necessarily a Sexologist (that horrible term is no choice or creation of mine). A poet who writes of daffodils is not compelled to be a botanical pundit. I agree with some lines of Edward Thomas on Words, lines happily cited by Mr. V. H. Collins in his book on *The Choice of Words*.

> You are light as dreams,
> Tough as oak,
> Precious as gold,
> As poppies and corn,
> Or an old cloak.

In a spirit of happily employed devotion I started to make word-anthologies. There were so many and such excellent anthologies of prose and poetry that it seemed ridiculous to tramp once more in that frequented field. But what had not been done, or not sufficiently done, was to survey words, to smell them out, and to handle or regard them as though they were Thomas's poppies and corn, acorns and oak trees. So I went about the business as an amateur in the full sense of the word, with nothing but my own personal reading in which to find the material and with an abiding relish for the tricks of verbal invention that articulate man has brought to the business of relating useful facts and telling useless stories. Of course the dictionaries had to be consulted and I have much for which to thank them. Once on the way I found the many 'helpers and servers' who continually pointed out some new and shining thing.

Those who have chiefly helped me have been mentioned with gratitude: I am sorry if there are any omissions or errors. In excuse of my mistakes I would ask the reader to consider the note on Squiggle in this volume.

One of my first words (in alphabetical order) is alamodality, the pursuit, even the worship, of fashion. Alamodality, I have concluded, is almost as powerful at the writer's or the official's desk as it is at the draper's and milliner's counter. Once a word has been tried and liked, it becomes as popular as a film-star whom all the companies are trying to buy at once. Then, like film-stars, they are dropped. At one time you could scarcely read a sentence about public affairs without discovering much about bottle-necks. At the time of writing, the alamodalists are very busy with pilot. For example, I read in my paper this morning about 'an agreement reached in Buenos Ayres yesterday under which the Argentine undertakes to supply 250,000 tons of meat next year at a "pilot" price of £161 a ton ... The "pilot" price is the figure for the best quality beef shipped frozen'.

What does this mean? If the figure of £161 is experimental, why not say so? Why drag in, so absurdly, the pilot? For if anybody is not an experimenter, it is he. The pilot is the man who knows every detail of the estuary and the harbour mouth by long study and experience and can therefore steer a vessel in without making any guesses or experiments whatever. He is the man of routine, the man on whom one relies. Yet he is dragged out to represent in our newspapers the spirit of experiment and the testing of schemes to see how they are likely to work out. This misuse of the word pilot is as silly as the incessant misuse of the word executive to suggest a tremendous fellow who makes important decisions. But an executor (or executive) is just the reverse. His name comes from the Latin for to follow and his job is to follow the instructions of the testator in the case of a will and certainly not to make any decisions of his own without the authority of the will and of the lawyers employed to interpret that document. I have mentioned this before, but the allure of executive as suggesting demonic energy, swift, original decisions, and enormous power is obviously very popular: the verbal alamodality of our time is on its side. Just as I was reading about the 'pilot' price of beef, I saw a letter to the Press about stories in women's magazines. The writer, who was answering complaints about those stories and explaining how they were chosen, signed himself, on behalf of one of the large magazine-producing firms, 'Fiction Executive'. Editor, evidently, was not good enough for him.

Each year now the gay and ingenious Fourth Leaders in *The Times* are reprinted in volume form. Here are found the highest levels of English prose composition; grace and wit are most happily mingled to ease our morning's introduction to news and views of a heavier kind. Yet the alamodality of certain terms infects even this range of essay-writing. One finds 'briefed' used where 'told' would be quite sufficient. 'One has to be told the way' is surely better than 'One has to be briefed as to the way'. But brief is a vogue-word of the moment. The absurd use of bracket in relation to figures survives too in these essays. 'Males in the shaving age bracket.' Why not 'males of shaving age'?

There is no one wholly guiltless of grammatical and syntactic errors and misuse of words. Mr. Vallins in his *Good English* has shown how fallible are the august. One need not go to the Comic Strip for cruelty to prose. I am myself more aggrieved by misuse of words than by misconstruction of sentences. But I do not wish to wander off into grumbles and to end upon a note of outraged austerity. I am not opposed to long and sonorous words as such; I only complain when the word is chosen not because of its size and splendour but because of its pomposity and its supposed power to persuade the simple reader that the writer is a mighty fine person. Those who would chase polysyllabic words, Grecians and Latinities, out of the language must show some sense of proportion. The great writer knows when to thunder at length and when to whisper briefly. So, in my selection, the reader will find some approved monsters as well as darling monosyllables. We have need of them all in their place.

Here is my list of recent correspondents: to these word-lovers I send my renewed thanks for the trouble they have taken and for the curious beauties and oddities to which they have so often led me.

Mrs. Janet Ashbee

J. H. Banbury
A. D. Baxter
George J. Beaudoin
Moncure Biddle
R. B. Blance
Stephen Bone
Leonard Brockington
John Brooks
R. G. Bultitude
W. M. Burton

Miss V. J. Chapman
Donald Barr Chidsey
Mary Child
Margaret Cole
R. Coleman
V. H. Collins
Philip Conklin
Michael R. Crump

Laurence Drury
Janet Dunbar
L. F. Dunn

F. Edmundson

Christopher Fostone

G. Gallie
Daniel George
Helen Grundy

Lionel Hale
H. Hardy
J. W. Hely-Hutchinson
George Henschel

Guy Innes

P. Shaw Jeffrey
W. F. Jeffrey

E. Muriel Kettle
H. J. Kettle
G. Norman Knight

John T. Lawrence
Mollie Leeper
S. Lees
John Lunan

Angus Macdonald
Dr. J. W. McFeeters
W. W. Maclellan
Maurice Macmillan
G. D. Malone
John Moore
M. Morley

G. N. G. Orsini

James G. Platt
G. Potter

David F. Rodger
Rev. John Rosie
Dr. A. Ross
H. Russell-Snook

John Shaw
W. H. Shepherd
Mrs. M. A. Simmons
Thomas H. Sims
James Slack
Alan Stark
Sir Ronald Storrs
H. W. Stubbs

Katherine Thicknesse
Mrs. M. P. Thomson
Stephen Trimen

G. H. Vallins
Judson Voyles

Stella A. Walker
J. F. Whitehead
C. A. Williams
J. W. Williams

Norman Young

To the Verbal Authorities,
coupled with the
name of
Eric Partridge

A WORD IN EDGEWAYS

ALAMODALITY

I HAD just come across this noun meaning fidelity to fashion when I encountered the following observations of Margaret Cavendish, Duchess of Newcastle. They occurred in her *Sociable Letters* (1664).

> Most Men and Women in this age, in most Nations in Europe, are nothing but Mode, as Mode-Minds, Mode-Bodies, Mode-Behaviour, Mode-Cloaths, Mode-Pastimes and Vices. . . .

The complaint holds and probably always will. To be, as the Communists say, a Deviationist (why not Deviator?) means effort and even audacity. The totalitarians delight in shaping the Mode-Mind and people less intense and less political are usually addicted to Mode-Cloaths. It is always surprising to me how far the brave-new-worlders, who deem themselves to be ahead of the news and the views, are in the grip of alamodality. Present them with a new artist or a new -ism and they are Mode-Cults, as the Duchess would have said, to the last devotee.

Women of social ambition like to be ahead of the mode and thus to make it. There ought to be some such word as premodality to describe their eagerness to be seen, discussed and followed. Men are rarely premodalists and are sometimes supposed to be contemptuous of alamodality altogether. But at the time of writing, the return of the bowler hat, which is no beauty, is making some progress with the young men to be seen in St. James's Street. Moreover, the Duke of Edinburgh has been photographed at Balmoral in what seems to be the Edwardian Norfolk Jacket and in the knickerbockers described as Plus Twos (i.e. not so long and baggy as Plus Fours once fashionable with golfers). This has caused, so my evening paper tells me, a demand for this attire by our alamodalist sportsmen of the country houses. This is a notable victory for Plus Twos, which had come to be rather dismally associated with late-Victorian cyclists, Mr. Ramsay MacDonald, and early Socialists attending Summer Schools.

But alamodality has had other elegances in its time. After the Restoration an alamode was 'a thin, glossy black silk hat'; later on, in the Victorian epoch, the rich man's tile had become the poor man's tuck-in. The Alamode was then a satisfying stew of beef and gravy and had its own kind of cook-house or restaurant. The young and hungry Charles Dickens knew the allure of a steamy window on a cold day with Alamode written across the panes or over the door. I suppose the Duchess of Newcastle would have called the hungry patrons swarming round an Alamode 'nothing but Mode-Mouths'.

ALCOHOL

ALCOHOL is a word ugly enough to suit those who insist on describing the drinking of a good wine as 'consuming alcohol'. Perhaps, therefore, it is just that this common and deterrent term for strong drink should come from the Moslem world in which it is abhorred.

Our 'al' words are often Arabians since 'al' is Arabic for 'the'. Al kohl was the powder. We do not drink powder, except as medicine. But powders were got by a process of rubbing and distillation similar to the methods by which spirits were obtained from plants and fruits. The kohl was rubbed on the eyelids; the spirit was imbibed by the heathens outside the dominion of Allah. The Arabians, who thus loaded us with the word alcohol, were learned men and gave us, in addition, alchemy, algebra, alkali and almanac. Alkali came from the ashes taken from the fire which did cooking by heating the utensils. So Potash is our alkali.

ANGUILLE

CONSULTING the dictionary about anguine to see whether it had any connection with anguish – it has not, meaning snaky or snake-like only – I noticed Anguille. The astonishing definition of this is 'A sort of small worms cast up by sick hawks'. Only by hawks? What about distressed eagles, bilious buzzards, and dyspeptic peregrines, pigeon-crammed? The word anguille, with this meaning, must appeal to artists of all kinds when suffering under the slights of silly criticism – silly, at least, as the victim sees it. For to the artist the peevish assessor is no better than a sick hawk and his judgments are no more than the vomited pellets of a queasy stomach. The London *New Statesman* once had literary critics of renown both of whom wrote a weekly article under pseudonym; both had birds of prey in their titles. One was Solomon Eagle and the other Affable Hawk: the former was J. C. Squire, the latter Desmond MacCarthy (both knighted later). The affability was shared. Neither looked round his book-shelf in order to find something to hate. Like all critics they had occasionally to censure, but neither discharged a weekly dose of wormwood or denounced any author who found the world still beautiful, the grass still green, and laughter permissible. In short, these birds threw up no anguilles.

BACHELOR

'THE world must be peopled. When I said I would die a bachelor I did not think I should live till I were married.' Nowadays most of us believe that much further peopling of the world would be a menace; we should not press Benedick's repentant doctrine. But let that pass. By Shakespeare's time the unmarried had settled down to their enduring titles of spinster and bachelor.

The bachelor began, it seems, as the owner or tenant of a grazing farm (bacca being a form of vacca, the cow). Why did he then become 'a young knight who followed the banner of another, a novice in arms'? Here's social promotion. Why, too, was the term transferred to civilian and academic life? That the bachelor's degree at a University should be lower than the master's or doctor's is a natural consequence of the notion of a novice. But that the baccalarius should become baccalaureus seems to have been due to a pun on laurel, symbol of success. I like the ring of 'baccalaureate sermon', an address to a just graduated class, though I surmise it can have been a considerable bore upon occasions.

We have wandered far from the pasture and the milking-shed. Bachelor is a nice, sturdy word and suggests good living. Why should Bachelor's Fare be only 'bread and cheese and kisses'? Kisses, yes: but no beef and beer? Bachelors profit by paying for one person only. So they should be able to do themselves well, as John Ford pointed out in some not very poetical poetry.

> A bachelor
> May thrive by observation on a little;
> A single life's no burthen; but to draw
> In yokes is chargeable and will require
> A double maintenance.

In Great Britain those who 'draw in yokes' are chargeable for double maintenance of the Treasury, if the wife has, or earns, money and so the tax-yoke is a crushing one. Yokes have brought us back to that dairy farm whence the bachelor so queerly springs. Let us leave him with his kine.

BANANA

NOTICING in a Serenade by Douglas Grant Duff Ainslie the enticing first two lines

> Lady of the lovely thighs
> Curving like banana fruit

I wondered why bananas have been so little present in our poetry. They are as suave in sound as in flesh. Why should peaches and cherry-ripe and apple-of-the-eye have such powerful positions in the vocabulary of affection? Obviously one would not look for a banana-tinted cheek, but for sweetness and richness there is surely a happy image for the love-lyricist in a ripe banana. (I refer to the small, tender Malayan species, the pesang, not to the great coarse fellow that has too much and too crudely represented this noble name in the British market.)

Emerson did pass an observation on bananas,

> The highest civility has never loved the hot zones.
> Where snow falls there is usually civil freedom;
> Where the banana grows, man is sensual and cruel.

But this dubious generalization on that stalest of school-room essay themes, the Influence of Climate upon Character, does not affect the succulence of the banana or the pleasure of rolling its name, as well as its substance, on the tongue. A popular song of 1923, 'Yes, we have no bananas, we have no bananas today', could hardly have achieved its great favour with a fruit of less engaging sound. 'Yes, we have no pine-apples.' That would never do. Bananas, which, had they been known, would have been eagerly snatched by the Latin poets to end their hexameter lines demanding the syllabic close of short-long-long, have been ridiculously neglected by our minstrels. There is a fine roll about them. Stage crowds, when called on to make tumultuous and revolutionary noises, are generally supposed to mutter or shout 'Rhubarb, Rhubarb' as a suitable noise. I think the producer might throw in some bananas for variety.

In his famous and exquisite 'Song of the Emigrants in Bermuda' Andrew Marvell attributed to the island oranges, pomegranates, figs, melons, and apples; how accurately, I do not know, since I have never been able to afford a holiday in that sunning-ground of the leisured and the wealthy. While he was being as lavish as this, he might well have thrown in bananas. Their music has been left to our barrow-boys – and the wise Mr. Ainslie. Also to fashion-writers and advertisers of 'alamodalities' for women. They sometimes employ the word banana as a colour. 'In nigger, wine, or banana.'

BANDIT

IT is odd to find this remark in the early seventeenth century. 'Banditti do you call them? I am sure we call them plain thieves in England.' That is just what we do not do now, for the Press loves to call smash-and-grab men bandits. The original banditti were outlaws, driven desperate by their exile from society. Forests and lonely roads were their haunts, not the frequented streets.

> Great men die oft by vile besonians;
> A Roman sworder and banditto slave
> Murdered sweet Tully; Brutus' bastard hand
> Stabb'd Julius Caesar: savage islanders
> Pompey the Great: and Suffolk dies by pirates.

This from *Henry VI*. We promote our thieves by calling them bandits. The cosh boy is raised to the society of great assassins.

Besonians or bezonians were first needy soldiers landed in Italy from Spain, then any kind of penurious beggar or rapacious outlaw. 'Under which king, Bezonian? Speak or die!' cried Pistol when he brought the news into Gloucestershire that Prince Henry the madcap was now King Henry the Fifth. The 'nips and foists' of the Boar's Head did poorly by that promotion.

We have taken other scoundrels from Italy. The eighteenth century knew its 'scrocconi', elegant sharpers and 'spivs'. Those who made the Grand Tour, risking banditti, with ciceroni looking out for tips and commissions and scrocconi in waiting to plunder them at their pleasures, added to their own vocabulary while they diminished their possessions.

BANG

WHILE reading some recently published American stories I came across the employment of the word bang to mean a lock (or shock) of hair on the forehead. The usage seems more common in America than in Britain. The bang was cut square over the brow, and the term is used of a horse's tail as well as of a human being's forelock. Not only horses could be bang-tailed. There were the anglers' flies as well. ' "These bang-tailed little sinners any good?" said Drysdale, throwing some cock-a-bondies across the table.' – *Tom Brown at Oxford*. ('Cockabondy' apparently comes from the Welsh '*coch a bon ddhu*, "*red with black stem.*" An angler's artificial fly.') (To 'take time by the bang' would be a serviceable way of describing swift and vigorous action. But does Father Time have his tresses cut square in front?)

The better-known bang was a blow long before it became a noise. Does 'bang went saxpence' refer to the Scotsman's slamming of the coin on the counter or to the explosion and consequent dispersion of that piece of property? Another kind of bang is 'a sudden impetuous movement' and so was a term for energy and what is now called 'pep'. To describe a man as full of bang is no bad way of suggesting a dynamic individual. 'Everything went with a bang' seems to sum up all the meanings of bang, except that of the square-cut frontal 'hair-do'.

BETWOTTLED

FAMILIAR by now are the three adjectives, all beginning with 'b', used to describe a person in a state of distraction. Of this trinity bewildered is the last. A place might be found in this company for betwottled. 'Some of the quadrupedes are betwottled' appears in the Verney papers. (If we can have centipedes with an 'e' why not quadrupedes? This suggests a larger and more formidable beast than does quadrupeds.) I have been criticized for saying that nappy was an adjective applicable to a restive and possibly betwottled horse; the nappy one, I am assured, is not so much frisky as froward: it is thrawn, as the Scots would say, refusing to move in the wanted direction and preferring to go home. In short it is nostalgic, in the correct sense of that much abused word. It may be surmised that the meaning of nappy varies in different parts of the country. Betwottlement, apparently, is the state of being bewitched or frenzied. Betwottled reminds one vaguely of bottled, in its slang sense of inebriated. A well-dined man could be just as fairly betwottled as is a horse with an imp of mischief in its temper.

BLEAR

DO small, aggressive children still put out the tongue as a symbol of rudeness, a parallel exercise to the cocking of snooks and the Elizabethan biting of defiant thumbs? This kind of challenge was once called blearing the tongue. But blear is twice a verb since it was both (intransitive) to have moist eyes and (transitive) to dim or deceive the eye. I came across it in Milton's *Comus.* Both as an adjective for blurred and as a verb to cozen with illusion it was a favourite of his. And rightly; for it powerfully suggests a rheumy obstruction and darkening of the sense.

Now we have for the most part limited blear to being a component of the adjective blear-eyed, but it might be happily preserved as a verb with a meaning rather stronger than that of blur. A sky bleared with smoke or a face bleared with weeping creates a more vivid apprehension of the smirching process than does a blurred heaven or blurred cheeks. To say of an unmannerly or tedious fellow that he blears the entire company would give the right impression of a pestilent companion.

BONE-SET

THOREAU wrote that 'the stillness, solitude, wildness of nature is a kind of thorough-wort or bone-set to my intellect. This is what I go out to seek. It is as if I always met in those places some grand, serene, immortal, infinitely encouraging, though invisible, companion, and walked with him'.

The plant bone-set (or thorough-wort) has a strengthening and pervasive sound. The passage of the bony metaphor from body to plant and back to the mind is a curious one. Thoreau's usage might have been more taken up. There are so many forms of writing, as well as of natural solitude, which deserve the name of bone-sets. Dr. Johnson I would call the greatest of all intellectual bone-sets within my own reading.

BRAINBLATHER

MR. J. L. BAILES, a specialist in northern English dialects, is not hopeful about the future of the native terms and idioms on the farm, since we are all State-instructed in our agricultural techniques as well as in reading and writing and arithmetic. Writing in the Journal of the recently formed and much needed Lancashire Dialect Society he remarked:

> Already I have found that the various official pamphlets on how to build a cowshed have resulted in young farmers forgetting the names of parts of 'byres' such as *fothergang*, *skelboose*, *slatherstone*. The 'cowleech' gives place to the veterinary surgeon, and sheep die of liver fluke instead of *turnsick*, *stackers*, *stoddy* or *brainblather*.

Brainblather must never die; rather should it pass far beyond the farmyard. Surely some of the talks delivered to the more intellectual Conferences at Summer Schools might be classified so. And turnsick could well be the adjective in front of it.

BRIMSTONE

'AN early brimstone butterfly, drifting past him like a blown yellow leaf, stole his attention from the sparrow and set him fruitlessly speculating about the primitive anonymous poet of long ago who, seeing such things with a child's eye and a child's wonder, in those days when everything was new, had called it the butter-coloured fly and so given this name to all the airy tribe.'

This from John Moore's story, 'Midsummer Meadow', another of his vivid landscapes and conversation-pieces of the Elmbury and Brensham countryside. I had not realized that brimstone had named so large a kingdom. There is an irony in the accidents by which a word so often associated with hell-fire should have given a title to the fluttering beauties of the garden, symbols, it seems, of all ethereal innocence. But brimstone is sulphur.

> From his brimstone bed, at break of day,
> A walking the Devil is gone,
> To look at his snug little farm of the World,
> And see how his stock went on.

These and other lines in 'The Devil's Walk' seem to have been the result of a collaboration by Coleridge and Southey, since the *Oxford Dictionary of Quotations* allots the poem to both. Did it really need the alliance of these two brains of might to compose this rhyme? However that may be, it has the smack of sulphur.

Brimstone is not a terrifying word. Seen by itself and without reference to any chemical matters, it might pass for the name of an innocent and salubrious resort. Could not there be a Brimstone-on-Sea, complete with pier, concert-parties, swimming-pool, and tennis-courts? But I have always felt queasy at the sight of brimstone in print, thanks to the use of it as a medicament by Mrs. Squeers at Dotheboys Hall. Sulphur and treacle were there served as a breakfast deterrent and thrust, in one huge wooden spoon, into all the boys' mouths, whatever the size of the latter. This was followed by 'a brown composition which looked like diluted pincushions without the covers and was called porridge'. The porridge was accompanied by a thin wedge of brown bread, by means of which it was eaten. Thus consumed, amid the starvation and flagellation of Dotheboys, brimstone as a dose has acquired far more terror in my mind than brimstone as an element of the sulphurous flames of hell itself. Sulphur, indeed, has the more imposing sound and aspect.

Blow me about in winds, roast me in sulphur,
Wash me in steep-down gulfs of liquid fire!

Would not Othello's imprecation suffer sadly by the substitution of brimstone for sulphur? Sulphurous is the adjective Shakespeare shrewdly prefers when he is voyaging in the abyss. The pit and the fire were sulphurous to King Lear and so were the tormenting flames to Hamlet's father.

There was also a feminine noun. Brimstone in this case meant shrew. We meet her in Charles Johnstone's *Chrysal, or the Adventures of a Guinea*: 'I hate the law damnably ever since I lost a year's pay for hindering our boatswain's mate's brother from beating his wife. The brimstone swore I beat her husband, and so I paid for meddling.'

BOUNCE

THERE is so much of the bouncing ball in our games (the luck of the bounce in the case of a golf-ball, bunker-finding or bunker-evading, the viciousness of the bounce in body-line bowling at cricket, and so on) that we are apt to forget bounce as a lie.

Here is Goldsmith in his lines to Lord Clare in 'The Haunch of Venison'.

Don't I hear you pronounce
This tale of the Bacon a damnable Bounce?
Well, suppose it's a Bounce – sure a poet may try,
By a Bounce now and then, to get Courage to fly.
But, my Lord, it's no Bounce; I protest in my turn
It's a Truth.

Bounce, of course, means swagger and bluff. But in this case it is bluntly contrasted with truth. Shakespeare used bounce in three ways, of the porpoise tumbling in the seas, of explosive, blustering talk, e.g.

> He speaks plain cannon-fire, and smoke, and bounce

and of the jerky skipping movement which Justice Shallow attributed to 'the little quiver fellow' of Clement's Inn in the manipulation of his weapons. Now we warn a person not to be bounced or talked over into this action or that purchase. We have forgotten the lie direct of Goldsmith's bounce.

BROCADE

BUTTERFLIES came fluttering to us in that form owing to the yellowness of butter. Butter, as we realize in this Margarine Age, is a lordling when matched with that pearly substitute. Was it not set forth, as Bible readers are aware, in a lordly dish? So butterflies have been lordly, ducal, and even regal in their names. When did those names arrive? We do not find them in Elizabethan poets, as far as I can remember. When Lear proposes a quiet end laughing at 'gilded butterflies' he names no species, and Marcius, son of Coriolanus, the nasty boy who mammocked (tore up) captured butterflies, was also described as savaging a 'gilded' specimen, type unspecified. John Moore tells me that the entitling of butterflies began in the early eighteenth century. That was a period of grandeur on the surface of society and the butterflies accordingly have grandiose titles to match their colouring, Purple Emperor, Duke of Burgundy, Queen of Spain, and Royal William, now better known as the Swallow-tail.

More plebeian, adds this same informant, and most attractive are the moth-names given by the old entomologists.

> Maiden's Blush, the Pease Blossom, the Poplar Lutestring, the Brownline Bright-eye (not to be confused with the Brightline Brown-eye, which was a different species altogether!) the Argent-and-Sable, the Beautiful Brocade, the Ruddy Highflier, the Blotched Emerald, the Marbled Coronet and even the Beautiful Snout!

All these appealing titles have other suggestions for me. The Marbled Coronet is obviously an unknown adventure of Sherlock Holmes. Both the Maiden's Blush and the Ruddy Highflier must be cocktails. What of the Beautiful Brocade – a story, perhaps, of the Yellow Bookish, Oscar Wilde period and style? The title certainly sets the scene in which Lord Arthur Savile might sip a cup of morning chocolate or later pour into a glass of curious crystal an exotic liqueur of purple, exquisitely pale.

Brocade is one of the most attractive of our fabric words. Most of these come from the towns where they were chiefly woven, e.g. Cretonne, Mantua, Kersey, to choose from three separate countries. But brocade means embossed, worked in a raised pattern. The sound of it to me is pure limelight and grease-paint, and calls up rich memories of Lewis Waller. Surely his 'Monsieur Beaucaire', the play that never failed him, however often he revived it, might have had a sequel called Beau Brocade, with further adventures among the elegance of Bath.

It has the right ring for the heroic verse of the epoch.

> Whether the Nymph shall break Diana's Law
> Or some frail *China* jar receive a Flaw.
> Or stain her Honour or her new Brocade,
> Forget her Prayers or miss a Masquerade –

Pope's Nymph takes us back to butterflies.

BRUNONIAN

ANYBODY called Brown must take an interest in the formidable adjective Brunonian. One of the numerous John Browns, a medical doctor of the eighteenth century, propounded a theory, called Brunonian, that all illness derives from excess or deficiency of excitement and must be treated with stimulants or sedatives. I wonder what the doctor prescribed for rheumatism or lumbago. Was the victim to be dosed into enthusiasm and so lured into skipping and dancing or doped into an apathy so intense that he forgot his racking pains? Brownism, as efficient students of *Twelfth Night* are able to inform their examiners, is a Puritan form of Church Government. This may have kept its zealots sufficiently excited to pass the Brunonian test. Brown studies were originally gloomy ones, brown being the equivalent of sombreness. But they seem to have lost their early melancholy and taken on the attractive quality of idle dreaming. The Brunonian sedatives might have induced such studies in those too much given to giddiness of fancy and exhilaration of temper.

BULSE

HORACE WALPOLE used the word bulse in discussing the case of Warren Hastings and his gains. It was a term for a package of jewels or of gold-dust and the dictionaries connect it with burse. A burse or borse was a leather purse before it became a business meeting-place or Exchange. The Bursar has remained with us in academic establishments, administering the intake and out-goings of the collegiate bulse or burse.

Bullion is a *bouillon*; it is the product of the boiling or melting which took place in a mint. The gold-dust of a bulse might thus be compounded into the bars or coins which are bullion. Bullion is a fine, solid word: you feel that you can rely on it to the end like a bulwark. A bulse might easily be lost or dispersed; but a decent quantity of bullion could only be lifted by a most determined gang of bully-ruffians.

BURDALONE

A SOLITARY person. The burd was at one time, says *O.E.D.*, 'a poetic name for woman, and may be equated with bird'. The Psalmist was a burdalone of this kind, when he proclaimed in his affliction,

I am like a pelican of the wilderness:
I am like an owl of the desert.
I watch, and am as a sparrow alone
upon the house top.

Bird, as a term for young ladies, now rather suggests gaiety and company than sadness and solitude. Birds of this feather are rarely burdalones.

The similes applied to fair ones and to best beloveds include the humblest. Mouse was for many years a man's term of endearment for wife or mistress. Shakespeare and Wycherley used it so. But Shakespeare had the sparrow also on his lovers' list. 'She fetches her breath as short as a new-ta'en sparrow', said Pandarus of 'prettiest villain' Cressida and in commendation of that flighty lady. I wonder whether the sparrows of the poets were the grubby urban finch that we know. It is true that we hardly ever see a sparrow decently clean. If we did so, we might consider the cock prettily umbered and the hen possessed of a delicate grey-brown. The Psalmist's roof-top sparrow may have been ours, but I feel sure that the

Passer, deliciae meae puellae

of Catullus was a green-finch or gold-finch and not our drab cock-sparrow of the kerbs and the gutters.

If I was a young woman I would sooner be called mouse than sparrow; the former's colour is more delicate, its behaviour more modest. Both, it must be confessed, are philoprogenitive and survive and multiply by their addiction to mating. The sparrow is no burdalone.

Another famous sparrow was that of John Skelton, Philip Sparrow, 'so pretty a fool, It would sit on a stool'. Philip, like Cressida and Cleopatra in the larger world, was given to panting and that adorably.

And prettily he would pant
When he saw an ant;
Lord, how he would pry
After the butterfly.

Skelton's emphasis on his Philip's prettiness compels me to think that he too was a green-finch or a gold-finch and not our sombre gutter bird.

BUZZ

BUZZ has more meanings than the usual one of humming and droning. To Shakespeare it was an exclamation of impatience or disgust; to Thackeray it was a verb for to empty, applied to a bottle. That, perhaps, links up with the slang usage of to buzz as to rob. Chariot-buzzers was an old term for those who snatched purses in public vehicles. When Marie Lloyd sang her famous song of a home broken up

> My old man said, 'Follow the van
> And don't dilly-dally on the way'

she used, during the patter, to look in her purse, find nothing there, and say, 'Girls, I've been buzzed.' Coming from one who was already on the tramp, this was, on the lips of a genius, as terrible as a line in *King Lear*.

The meaning was obvious, but the word was quite new to me when I heard it. It is likely that the phrase 'buzzing a bottle of port' meant robbing it of its contents: table-buzzers, not chariot-buzzers, would be responsible for that. I never hear the word buzz connected with stealing in the slang of today, but it may linger on in the relics of the Cockney language.

The word has also been used as an adjective meaning swollen. In *A Supplementary English Glossary* (1881), by T. Lewis O. Davies, M.A., Vicar of S. Mary Extra, Southampton, I find: 'The Anti-jacobin having spoken of P—r's [Parr's] *buzz* prose, adds in a note: "The learned reader will perceive that this is an elegant metonymy, by which the quality belonging to the outside of the head is transferred to the inside. *Buzz* is an epithet usually applied to a large wig. It is here used for swelling, burly, bombastic writing." '

CALCITRANT

WHY not, I have been asked, use calcitrant for the man who is not recalcitrant, a complaisant (not complacent) man, one who will accept the counsel of reason and refuses to be contumacious? I have an affection for contumacious, sometimes confused with contumelious; contumacy, which is Miltonic, belongs to the high lingo of defiance. Calcitrant, as a matter of fact, already exists with permit of the lexicon, but it does not mean the opposite of recalcitrant. It means the same thing, but in rather less degree. To calcitrate is to kick back and to recalcitrate is to emphasize the backness, possibly the backside, that is contumaciously kicked. If a calcitrant fellow needs discipline, a recalcitrant needs it more.

Further questions from the same source. Why cannot we have transigent men for the sweetly reasonable who will take a middle course? There seems to be no reason why we should not admit the virtue of transigence. Intransigence, however, came to us from Spain, where sweet reasonableness is not common. The politicians are of the Left or of the Right: the liberals of the middle are scarce. Los Intransigentes, who gave us our word Intransigents, were the men of the extreme Left, and in Spain the Right has its extremity too. So we never heard of Los Transigentes. The liberal-minded might demand a British recognition of the word transigence. But we have reasonableness and moderation already.

CALOMEL

THIS is the most musical of the purges. Little wonder that Reginald Bunthorne, the Fleshly Poet of *Patience*, had it in his voluptuous vocabulary.

> What time the poet hath hymned
> The writhing maid, lithe-limbed,

Quivering on amaranthine asphodel,
How can he paint her woes,
Knowing, as well as he knows,
That all can be set right with calomel?

Bunthorne further refers, in his list of ingredients and 'uncompounded pills' to aloes and colocynth. The last is coloquintida, the bitter-apple. Some notable terminology had reached the bottom of a purgative draught by Bunthorne's time. Macbeth knew only of rhubarb and senna: Iago knew that coloquintida was bitter, but he does not speak of it as an evacuant.

Calomel, which is mercurous chloryde, means Black Beauty. T. H. Savory, in *Browsing Among Words of Science*, says that there is a considerable choice of more or less improbable anecdotes to explain why mercurous chloryde, that spur to sluggish livers, was honoured with an attribution of beauty. 'The most often quoted', he states, 'concerns a "whymsical chymist" who employed a Negro assistant in his laboratory and was wont to refer in this word to his beautiful complexion. This explanation is at least as old as Chambers' Dictionary of 1727.' Whether we believe that or not, the sound of calomel is as refreshing as the effects of it are intended to be.

CARAPACE

'THE upper body-shell of tortoises and crustaceans.' So fair a sound deserves a gentler meaning. Since Cara is the Latin for dear one, then surely a darling who covers a lot of grass, as the comedians say of the fast feminine, might seem to be indicated by a carapace. The 'cara' words are so handsome and have such alien charm that this rough and tough invader of their niche in the lexicon distresses me. Steeds of mettle caracole and may have dashing carabineers upon their soaring and unrestful backs. Travellers to the gorgeous East would in past centuries thread the coral islands in Caracores or Caramoussals; to read of such journeys is an occupation made the sweeter by the suction of caramels. I discover that a cannon at billiards was known of old by its Spanish name of Carambole. This was applied both to noun and verb so that caracoling horses might carambole in the process. Amid so much of romance the stiff and shelly meaning of carapace is indeed disappointing.

But I was brought to it by a glorious passage in a Paper on the Navel (more correctly 'A study of the Umbilicus') by the late Dr. O. H. Mavor ('James Bridie' to the playgoer). Mavor's argument, which will be congenial to most of us, was that man's natural function is repose. He explained that the word navel means the hub of a wheel, and round it we rotate. We are both centripetal and centrifugal and his discourse, he admitted, was of the latter kind, a random and outward-flying matter. In the course of these centrifugal observations he noted that Man

> can lie on his back, a posture long sustained by no other uncarapaced animal except in death. It is little wonder that his sleep is the amazement of the animal kingdom. It is superior to the long unconsciousness of hibernating animals. They curl their vegetative organs into the smallest bulk and lie in an uncomfortable tight knot in a condition near to death. How different is man! Man's great lungs heave and blow, his noble heart thuds merrily, and his marvellous bowels continue in gentle peristalsis, his brain is the house of a thousand lovely fancies, his liver, his blood, his glands, transform the dead cells of his food into the living elements of his body and slay his myriad of airy foes. He is badly constructed for locomotion by road or by tree. The slowest fish swims faster. He is adapted primarily for rest.
> This and much more to the same purpose we can learn from the contemplation of the umbilicus or navel.

So let all of us who are torpid, indolent, and little given to violent motion take heart. Inertia is an important aspect of our natural genius. Among the great host of the Uncarapaced we are the master-sleepers, and in reclining we do but comply with our destiny.

Having become entangled in the umbilical cord, which is Latin, we can hardly escape without a glance at the omphalos, which was the Greek word for the same, and held by Dr. Mavor to be the nobler of the two. He gave his reason.

> Professor Popochik, the etymologist, tells us that omphalos means the drawing together of the band of the helmet that held the crest or plume. The pleasant picture of a spray of feathers springing from the umbilicus of each of us need not detain us. I wish to draw your attention to the sonority of the word 'omphalos', and to regret, in passing, that Celsus thought fit to change the noble-sounding name of a noble organ to the pedestrian word 'umbilicus'.

It is well known that the navel has powers of mystical fascination. An Omphalopsychite is 'one of a sect of quietists who practised gazing at the navel as a means of producing hypnotic reverie'. (Presumably it was his own navel at which the omphalopsychite stared so rewardingly.) This centralized concentration is part of the Yogi practice and may lead to calm and wisdom. But for a sheltered life a good strong shell may be helpful. It is not only the crustaceans who have discovered that. Not so long ago Britons scuttled, in their tin hats, to a Morrison or Anderson shelter, precious carapaces of their metallic kind.

CARAVAN

BEING large and clumsy I have never felt anything but horror at the prospect of living in a caravan, a vehicle intended for the small and tidy. But the word is perfectly designed to lure the romantic to the open road.

> The Stars are Setting and the Caravan
> Starts for the Dawn of Nothing – oh make haste.

The Dawn of Nothing sadly sums up so many of our ideas and aspirations and so much of our fondest enterprise: but to travel thither in a caravan is at least a compensation, making music for the ear.

The famous

> Where my caravan has rested
> Flowers I leave you on the grass

was part of a song by Edward Teschemacher whose dulcet melody so soothed our parents and won such vast popularity that Caravans became almost a jest. But housing shortage, the high cost of hotels and holidays, and the convenience of a motor-car to pull it has made the caravan one of the most frequent occupiers of the summer road. The Persian karwan has travelled far – and now is frequently in motion.

The caravan was originally not a vehicle, but a company of merchants or pilgrims with their transport. It could also be a fleet of ships. (They, too, have started for the Dawn of Nothing.) Later it was limited to the covered wagon, the house on wheels. The caravanserai was the inn with a large court for the 'parking' of caravans. Its descendant is now, very often, a field where large numbers of these mobile lodgments are collected with, one hopes, a water-supply and some modicum of sanitation. As seen on the fringe of 'beauty spots' or of the sea-coast the contemporary British caravanserai has no attractions for me. Omar's Caravanserai had known Sultans in their Pomp. But our examples tend to acquire a considerable air of squalor.

Yet the caravan, because of the romantic rumble in its name, becomes almost a magical chariot in a lyric. Ralph Hodgson's

> Time, you old gipsy man,
> Will you not stay,
> Put up your caravan
> Just for one day?

profits by its spell. But nothing short of total rooflessness will persuade me to be cribbed in this contraption, however elegant the fittings. Room in which to move and stretch and be untidy is my first demand of a habitation.

CENTRIC

I AM so often asked about negative adjectives that have no positive, or a positive only very rarely used, i.e. disgruntled and dishevelled, that I naturally keep an eye open for them. What of eccentric, which is now more frequently applied to mental than to spatial movement? The adjective centric has been used in the past as an alternative to central, but it is rare today and has never, as far as I know, been applied to intellectual affairs and types of opinion. The politicians and sportsmen use centre as an adjective. They have their Centre Parties and Centre Forwards. Centric, I think, could well be kept to signify the opposite of eccentric.

At a gathering which I attended recently for some discussion of the arts I felt that I was the only centric person present. This is not so conceited as it may sound. Centric is not for me the same as normal or sane; nor are eccentrics merely freakish. I do not suggest that my companions were crazy, but they were certainly somewhat vagabond in their views, wandering to curious conclusions which did not seem to have any philosophy or logical principles behind them. They had little or no use for any opinions but their own. The centric man I regard as having a settled and arguable position; he respects tradition and innovation without being a slave to either; he is ready to consider and discuss fairly all the fluctuating creeds of the eccentrics; he is unshaken by sudden winds of doctrine.

Moreover, he is not in the least impressed by long words, expecting that the eccentric who produces a new -ism or -ology should at least be able to state, within the comprehension of a normally educated person, exactly what he means. How often, incidentally, can the devotees of 'advance' do that? I remember being told by an essentially advanced producer of plays that he intended to present a piece in 'an Existentialist manner'. When I asked him what he meant by Existentialism he was completely unable to explain. Apparently he confused it with Surrealism. There is much need of a firmly set centricity when one is in company of that kind.

Eccentrics in social life may be so delightful as to be a necessity. British history has been rich in people who had 'brave notions' and would not conform, initiators of strange fashions, builders of 'follies'. May they persist. But we could hardly get along in a society where all had crinkum-crankum fancies. Eccentrics need their opposites. The centric, as I see him, is a man with a firm stance. But he also has an open mind.

CHAFFY

WHEN Palamon and Arcite, the Two Noble Kinsmen, come to words, in the play of that title by John Fletcher and, I am confident, William Shakespeare too, the former calls the latter 'a confest traitor', 'voydest of honour', 'falsest cosen', and finally 'a Chaffy Lord, Not worth the name of Villaine'. Chaffy, for worthless, seems almost weak amidst the general abuse. Nowadays we make so much fuss about having 'roughage' in our food that to call it chaffy might be a compliment. Indeed I can see it as the name of a new Breakfast Food, 'Start the Day Right With Chaffy.' 'Chaffy stimulates but never irritates. It coaxes you to inner health.' Or 'All the Family take All-Chaff.' But to the Elizabethans husks were for the swine and chaff, humanly speaking, was rubbish. 'Picked from the chaff and ruin of the times.' Perhaps they were right. Keats was on their side: everything, without his Fanny's company, was like 'chaff in the mouth'.

I had thought that the use of chaff for banter or tease was a trifle genteel. But the dictionary marks it as 'somewhat vulgar'. Surely the delicately bred heroine of a Victorian novel was permitted to chaff her companions?

CHEETIE

AMONG the numerous terms for a cat occurs, chiefly in Scotland and perhaps chiefly in the south-west of Scotland, cheetie, spoken usually as a term of endearment. Has it, I am asked, anything to do with cheetah, the Hindu name for the hunting leopard and certainly feline, but not easily lovable? Or is it connected with Clan Chattan, who were the sons of the epical Caledonian hero Cat and may have given their name to Caithness?

I have no answer. Cheetie may, after all, only be a softening of Kitten and Kitty. The naming of the domestic cat is mysterious, as befits an animal which, in maturity, is generally aloof and often has an air of other-worldly comprehension. Puss, for example, is unexplained. It is by no means the same as purr. Then there is malkin; but that is uncomplimentary, for the malkin was a slattern. To watch the progress of Coriolanus through the streets of Rome there was general press and self-bedizenment of the populace.

> The kitchen malkin pins
> Her richest lockram round her reechy neck.

Cheetie, whatever its origin, is kinder to cats and kittens than was malkin when the latter was transferred from the human to the animal world.

CHUFF

MY attention has been called, as people write to editors when they are proposing to bring a libel action against a newspaper and do not wish to admit that they read the accursed thing (which, of course, they do), my attention has been called, I repeat, to the various charms of the word chuff. Parson Woodforde was quoted: 'Neville Custance is a very chuff boy indeed as ever I saw, seemed displeased and cross with everything – would not eat a bit of Cake when brought to him.' There is further news that chuff is still so used in

Yorkshire. It has old usage as a noun elsewhere, meaning a boor of the ill-tempered kind.

But it also means a fat cheek: the sound of it is as apt to broad and beaming chops as it is to a surly-churly fellow. The adjective derived from this chuff is completely at variance with the gruff chuff and means first chubby and then pleased and happy. I hear that a lady from Nottingham spoke to my correspondent about a friend who was 'very chuffed about getting a bargain at the sales'. North of the Trent this might have meant that she was disgusted, not delighted, with her luck.

COCKY

COCKY for conceited is a piece of slang that now has a period look. There was once a verb to cock which meant to brag or swagger. Perhaps this came from cocking of the hat which could be a sign of defiance. 'Do you cock your hat at me, Sir?' was a parallel to the Shakespearean 'Do you bite your thumb at me, Sir?' (It is odd that the introduction of Sir can be made in such contradictory ways. It is frequently the companion of a challenge, even an insult. Watching a maul in a game of Rugby Football I have often heard one player use rude and even obscene words to another and then end his fury with Sir. Yet Sir is also deferential, sometimes formally and sometimes sincerely polite. Men of forty who are approached as Sir by those of twenty usually do not like this form of address; it turns them into reverend, and very senior, seniors.)

Cocky, I am told, is a common and quite friendly name for any stranger whom one meets in Australia, being used 'as the name Joe was used in England and as the name Mac is used in Canada'. There have been so many Scottish immigrants in Canada that this greeting of a stranger with Mac is natural. I do not think Joe is commonly thrown about in England nowadays, but Wilfred Pickles's very popular radio programme 'Have a Go, Joe' was an instance of using Joe, cordially, to salute all and sundry.

Australian cockatoos were trained to hail arrivals with 'Hello, Cocky'. My correspondent was so greeted when he went to visit Melba in her fine home outside Melbourne. Cockatoo or cocky farmers, he further suggests, were so called because they lived in the bush and scratched for a living. The Canadian parallel was to be owner of a gopher ranch, the gopher being a burrowing animal, rat, squirrel, or even land-tortoise, and a gopher-hole being a miner's digging made without much previous prospecting, in fact a pot-shot.

The other name applied by Australians to an English cocky has been pommy or apple-cheek, explained as a parallel to red-neck. People tanned by the sun or made pallid through living in smoky, cloudy places and spending most of their day in mills and factories are surprised to find 'the roseate hues of early dawn' upon a human countenance. Some Lancashire folk used to call Roman Catholic priests red-necks, presumably because some of them came over from a fresh-aired upbringing on Irish farms and had not yet been sicklied by a mill-town climate.

CONVALLARIACEOUS

THIS seven-syllabled giant suits the subject of Gracie Fields's well-known song, 'The biggest aspidistra in the world'. For convallariaceous is just what the aspidistra is. John Moore, who has acquired in England's Middle-West a treasury of native names for plants and beasts and insects usually known by more solemn titles, told me recently that the aspidistra is a lily. Much-loved for its tenacity, much-mocked for its Suburbanity – yes, this is a dictionary word – the aspidistra endures all our facetiousness with no bowing of the head. It sounds, with that Grecian spear (aspis) in the forefront of its name, far better than it looks. In its kinship it has distinction. Its convallariaceity comes from Lilium Convallium, lily of the valley. The Tennysonian 'lily-maid of Astolat' might as well have been called Aspidistra as Elaine. But there must be no abbreviation, if this is to become a favoured Christian (or given) name. Lady Aspidistra Vale will pass: 'Aspie, darling' is altogether too serpentine.

Our lily of the valley may ring a gentle bell and look like a poet's pet, but in essence it is severely medical, yielding Convallarimin, 'an acrid purgative glucoside'. I apologize for returning to the pills and potions so soon after my note on calomel. But I have been led up this garden, or green-house, path by Aspidistra whose medical possibilities have, perhaps, been insufficiently explored. Those feeling seedy and dumpish might profit internally by chewing the landlady's darling pot-plant and so taking a serviceable dose of Convallarimin, but that hostess would much prefer their recourse to calomel. If you can imagine yourself seeing Aspidistra in print for the first time, it might strike you not as a joke but as a handsome addition to the catalogue of floral felicities.

CRAPULOUS

WE have abandoned the classic crapula for the Anglo-Saxon hang-over. Both words have their merits; an image of somebody sea-green, catarrhal and peevish is well suggested by the adjective crapulous. Hang-over is a simpler statement of oppressive and depressive consequence. The eighteenth-century writers made frequent allusion to this unpleasant aftermath, and I have been reminded that Charles Cotton used it earlier still in his *Night Quatrains.*

> The drunkard now supinely snores,
> His load of ale sweats through his pores,
> Yet, when he wakes, the swine shall find
> A crapula remains behind.

Nowadays we treat the condition with aspirin, alka-seltzer, and other cooling alkaline swills. The Elizabethans used to take a light alcoholic draught to shake off the languor and the thirst of a heavy crapula. Christopher Sly, who should have known about this kind of therapy, demanded 'For God's sake a pot of small ale', and rejected, wisely, the suggestion of sack, when he woke up in the lordly bed-chamber. Mr. Pepys, after coming home 'foxed', drank chocolate in the morning, a frightening thought. But he, too, should have learned by experience.

The elegant English nobleman of the eighteen-eighties, if we accept the authority of Oscar Wilde, was not roused with a cup of tea but with chocolate, which is in the Pepys tradition. Lord Arthur Savile, after his nocturnal perambulation of the West End and Bloomsbury, 'sick with horror' at the prospect of the murder he must commit, woke at twelve.

> Then his valet brought him a cup of chocolate on a tray. After he had drunk it, he drew aside a heavy *portière* of peach-coloured plush, and passed into the bathroom. The light stole softly from above, through thin slabs of transparent onyx, and the water in the marble tank glimmered like a moonstone. He plunged hastily in, till the cool ripples touched throat and hair, and then dipped his head right under, as though he would have wiped away the stain of some shameful memory. When he stepped out he felt almost at peace. The exquisite physical conditions of the moment had dominated him, as indeed often happens in the case of very finely-wrought natures, for the senses, like fire, can purify as well as destroy.

Much power in onyx, marble and a cup of chocolate!

CRISPS

WE all eat 'crisps' on occasion, for these potato-wafers accompany the cocktail party at the Grand Babylon as well as being freely purchased in the packet at the Red Lion or Black Horse. They are so called, presumably, because they are hard, brittle and crunchy. But crisp, before it got this connotation of a crackling substance, had a strange variety of meanings. Shakespeare used it twice of water and once of the sky. The river Severn, affrighted by the conflict of Mortimer and Glendower,

> Ran fearfully among the trembling reeds
> And hid his crisp head in the hollow bank.

Crisp there probably means wavy and curly. Chaucer had used it so of hair. In the masque in *The Tempest* Iris bids the Naiades, 'nymphs of the wind'ring brooks', leave their crisp channels. Wavy again? Or clear? In *Timon of Athens* the raging outcast speaks of

> The abhorred births below crisp Heaven
> Whereon Hyperion's quickening fire doth shine.

This is generally interpreted as meaning bright and lucent. For crisp does mean shining elsewhere. But Shakespeare may have been thinking of white, wavy clouds like the ripples of the Severn and of Iris's channels.

From these heights we descend to crisp as a noun of the Kitchen, signifying the crackling of pork. So we move on to the potato crisps of common delight. A correspondent informs me that in West Cornwall it is common to misplace consonants. The word pixie, for fairy, becomes pisky (it used to be pisgy in Devon) and he assures me that 'in any inn around St. Just local inhabitants can be heard asking for a picket of crips'. I fancy that the smoothing out of crisps is not limited to St. Just or even to West Cornwall. Familiar words are apt to lose a letter or soften one. Trumps at cards are often called trumphs in the Glasgow area, where the player of an ace might exclaim 'Here it's' rather than 'here it is' when he puts it down. The Cockney is supposed to say srimps for shrimps and may very well ask for a packet of crips too. Crisps is a something of a nuisance to lazy speakers.

The potatoes sold in this slender form remind me of the name Smith. In the pictured 'comics' of my boyhood the Londoner's Smith was Smiff. Smiths Crisps, though familiar, invite some slurring from the eager or slightly fuddled consumer. 'A packet of Smiff's crips' might come easier. Shakespeare, writing before Sir

Walter Raleigh's importation had become popular, kept crisp for larger matters. Falstaff would certainly have disdained such trifling companions for his sherris-sack. The man who disdained eggs with his liquor ('I'll no pullet-sperm in my brewage') was not to be regaled with a sliver of a tuber. But Bardolph and the Page might have welcomed such a nibble when larger fare was lacking.

Mincing, who is Millamant's maid in *The Way of the World*, when explaining that her lady curled her hair only with letters written in poetry, wished to describe the result as crisp, but she called it crips. On being laughed at, she retorted, 'You're such a critic, Mr. Witwoud.' So the crisp-crips confusion is an old one.

CRUMPET

LORD ASQUITH of Bishopstone has appealed for more muffins to ease the strains of the afternoon and indeed of life itself. (And why should not a Lord of Appeal do a little appealing as well as being appealed to?) When told that Britain lacked butter to make his desired confections and so to refill the tray of the old-time muffineer and set the hand-bell ringing in the streets again, he asked why crumpets should be able to defy that shortage. He does not like crumpets. To him 'they are limp, lardaceous, pock-marked parodies of muffins'. With that he may be said to have put the crumpet in its place, which, for him, is out of the window.

I thought lardaceous must be an Asquithian creation. But the dictionary gives it protection, telling us that it means 'containing lardacein', and lardacein, defined, is certainly no matter for the queasy. It is 'a nitrogenous substance deposited under morbid conditions in certain minute arteries and tissues of the body'. Those 'morbid conditions' immediately avert my appetite: also I am surprised to find *O.E.D.* writing 'under' conditions: my instructors in English composition had always made it plain that we were in or amid certain conditions, not beneath them.

But let us return to our crumpets. They mean curved or curled up cakes, since to crump is to bend into a curve. But they are no more curvaceous – to use an adjective dear to the advertisement-writers for lingerie and such – than any other kind of circular bun. However, to crump has another meaning, 'to eat with an abrupt but somewhat dulled sound applied to horses and pigs'. And why not to the human crumpeteer, for surely we may munch abruptly but in a muffled way our lardaceous muffin-substitutes?

Incidentally, I surmise that Lord Asquith may have been inclined to this rage by a surfeit of crumpets in his youth. I remember that, at the Oxford College of which we were simultaneous members, it was customary to send out from the buttery at tea-time large piles, hot or lukewarm under a metal cover, of the extremely limp, lardaceous and pocked-marked enemies of his palate. These were often accompanied by an equally rich pile of banana sandwiches. The banana was so long away from our English menu that few now are aware that a sliced, well-ripened banana makes an excellent wadding for two thin slices of fresh, well-buttered bread. Teas were gigantic then, banana-bountiful and crumpet-lardy. But they came after exercise and lunch was scanty.

Slang has promoted crumpet, Lord Asquith doubtless dissenting, to the honour of representing the human head. This signification of the brain-pan it has shared with boko, napper, noggin, and nut among others. The nut is in the list for obvious reasons of shape, and the napper presumably because it is the site of one's nap or hair. Boko sounds like something attractive to bashers and crumpet, for skull or sconce, can be explained by yet another meaning of the verb to crump, that is to hit or slog. The crump as an explosive missile is a further product of that. It is a melancholy fact that we should regard the seat of intelligence chiefly as something to be bashed: but that, unfortunately, is what our slang terms for it do imply.

Daniel George, in *Pick and Choose*, quotes from Boswell's *Johnson* a story told by Topham Beauclerck: 'Mr. —, who loved buttered muffins, but durst not eat them because they disagreed with his stomach, resolved to shoot himself; and then he ate three buttered muffins for breakfast, before shooting himself, knowing that he should not be troubled with indigestion.'

In *A Peck of Troubles* Daniel George re-tells another muffin story – Crabb Robinson's: 'I have heard of a lady, by birth, being reduced to cry "muffins to sell" for a subsistence. She used to go out a-nights with her face hid up in her cloak, and then she would in the faintest voice utter her cry. Somebody passing by heard her cry – "Muffins to sell, muffins to sell! Oh, I do hope nobody hears me." '

CUMBER

CUMBER as a noun for trouble or distress has disappeared. Sir Walter Scott used it in his 'Coronach'.

> Fleet foot in the correi,
> Sage counsel in cumber.
> Red hand in the foray,
> How sound is thy slumber!

When I first noticed it I thought that it might be a Scottish version of chamber, since counsels, councils and chambers are so often linked together. The old spelling of corrie, the hollow in the mountain-side where the deer shelter and feed, is now as rare as is the use of cumber as a substantive. Why did this kind of cumber vanish while the verb remained? It is a useful, expressive word and we must all have felt some time that we were in a devil of a cumber.

I fail to see why James Hogg's couplet in a poem to a Skylark,

> Bird of the wilderness
> Blithesome and cumberless

should qualify for inclusion in that agreeable Anthology of Bad Verse, *The Stuffed Owl*. To me cumberless is an excellent adjective for the certainly soaring and presumably carefree bird in question. A note about Hogg's lines is added from the hand of Sir John Squire: 'A couplet which I believe, had it occurred in a work by a Babu, would have been treated as a rich example of comic English.' Why on earth? Presumably neither Sir John nor the ingenious editors of the Anthology, D. B. Wyndham Lewis and Charles Lee, knew of the old and excellent use of cumber for trouble and sorrow.

DADDOCKY

THIS from Gloucestershire to mean rotten, especially of wood. 'That's a daddocky gate-post.' Daddock gets into the dictionary as a country term for decayed wood. The adjective might well be kept and its use extended since both look and sound so well communicate its meaning. We talk of weedy youths to mean lanky and feeble ones: this is absurd since every gardener knows that many a weed is the toughest and most enduring of growths. Why not a daddocky lad? It also occurs to me, since I have been playing Bridge this evening, that I have held some daddocky hands and that, with bad luck added to indifferent play, I have been a daddocky partner.

DEBATE

THIS from Scotland and concerning Galloway.

> Some sixty or seventy years ago, the shepherd from the Back Hill was describing to my mother a fierce snow-storm of the previous winter; 'the sheep smoored in the drifts could mak nae debate ava . . .' Enchanting tho' the picture may be of snow-bound sheep sitting in conclave, I can only suppose that debate is connected with the French *se debattre* – they were unable to fight their way out. It is too good a phrase to be lost.

The French origin of this kind of debate is doubtless true. But the usage of the word to describe physical combat is not limited to bygone shepherds of the Back Hill o' the Bush in the loneliest reaches of the Lowland's Highlands, as Galloway can well be called. I found that the shepherd was in tune with Chaucer, 'His cote-armour in which he would debate', and with Sir Walter Scott, 'In many a well-debated field'. I suppose that Debating Societies occasionally restore the old conception of a discussion that is actually violent. There have been blows struck and books thrown in our own House of Commons, whereas the hurling of inkpots, in addition to arguments and abuse, has often been a part-time occupation in the French Chamber of Deputies. Street-corner debating round the soap-box platform has seen many a scuffle of limbs as well as tournament of tongues.

DEVONA

I DO not wish to seem the old fogey ever moaning over past delights, but I must none the less record a lamentation for the sweets that are no more – or are not easily discoverable. Similar substances, in moderated quantity, are, I suppose, still there. But the names dwindle. Caramels, it is true, abide, and their name suggests slow, sweet absorbency. But I remember from my boyhood Devona, a most succulent hard toffee that took a really long time to soften in the mouth and so, priced at a penny for a large cake, was a superb bargain. All the pinguitude of Devonian pasture was in it. The label was most apt. Devona could be topped off with a Cho-hone, which was a chocolate-covered cube packed with rich, gelatinous matter of many hues. We had some French reference in our tuck-shop vocabulary too. Chocolat Montelimar was nutty and sweet, Raspberry Noyeau was soft, succulent, and crimson, and there were the various types of Nougat, a name that still abides.

Contemporary entitling of sweets is sadly unromantic. A Peppermint Bullseye hits the target, but I am not allured by a Peppermint Lump. The Mars Bar is, to some extent, the deputy for the old

Cho-hone and I regard a Mars Bar affectionately as 'more than somewhat'; but its name is too martial, too staccato to describe one of the confectioner's pleasures of peace, an article both suave and substantial. When I go to Scotland I search for my old friends, 'Soor Plooms', but the sour plums, which were not sour at all, elude me. Turkish Delight never much delighted me: if I do not see much of it now, I do not feel that my palate is being cheated; but the name suggested a glorious self-indulgence.

DISCOUNTENANCE

'SMOKING is discountenanced.' Nor forbidden, I suppose. No penalty beyond a frown or a frosty glance. Or is this merely a pompous and supposedly polite description of a veto? I have never been so ill-mannered as to light up in face of the discountenancers. But in a spirit of curiosity somebody might light a cigarette in order to discover whether discountenancing is supported by sanctions, as the international lawyers would say, or whether it only provokes the glum glance, the scowl dismissive.

Discountenance is one of our popular evasions. Some people prefer to call themselves indisposed when they are ill; in the same way they feel it more dignified to discountenance than to forbid. For my part I discountenance the practice of calling a veto by a name at once pompous and hesitant.

DISGUSTING

IN an account of the first Duke of Wellington's funeral, written by the present Duke and published in *History To-Day*, I met a striking observation on the meaning of the word disgusting. The writer was referring especially to the Lying-in-State in the Great Hall of Chelsea Hospital from November 13th to 17th, 1852. The crowds wishing to attend were enormous and, since the police arrangements were at first wholly inadequate, they were unruly as well. One man and two women were actually crushed to death. 'It is interesting to note,' remarked the present Duke in his article, 'that both Charles Greville and Lord Douro use the word "disgusting" of the funeral arrangements.' Then he added, 'They used it in the same sense as Jane Austen used it, meaning what we should call "antipathetic". Disgusting is one of the few words in the English language which time has strengthened instead of weakening.'

Disgust, by origin, means contrary to one's taste rather than revolting. When Greville wrote after this occasion that all public funerals are disgusting he meant that they were not to his liking and offended his sense of propriety. Now we should interpret his statement as meaning that he found public funerals actually nauseating. Disgust, as a noun, usually in the plural, once meant quarrel, affront, or snub.

The adjective disgustful seems to have vanished: a pity, since to call a book or a play that is full of bad taste disgustful is justly descriptive. So disgusting remains, usually intensified by an adverb such as utterly, to signify the odious and revolting. But a century ago one could claim to have found so-and-so's company or such and such a dish disgusting without implying that the person was completely unbearable and the victuals rancid or otherwise impossible to consume. None the less, returning to the Great Duke, we may well imagine that the morbidity and tumultuous conduct of the crowds at Chelsea were disgusting in our sense as well as distasteful to Greville and Lord Douro.

DIVERT

THE use of divert as a noun was a favourite practice of Neil Munro's 'Erchie, My Droll Friend', Erchie of the flat foot and the warm heart. Erchie was a kirk beadle in Glasgow by day and a banquet waiter by night, and he found much in life to amuse him, many a 'divert'. Protesting against the nuisance of Kirk Sales of

Work run by women for women, he said: 'A man's bazaar wad be a rale divert; naethin' to be sold in't bit things for use – everything guaranteed to be made by men – and them tryin'!'

The meaning of divert is here a mixed one, including difference and fun. With that double significance the divert is a very happy term. Deviation has become a crime in Communist countries; but among free men most forms of it are welcome; our eccentrics are often the most desirable diverts.

Congreve's Millamant would not, in the physical sense, deviate. 'I nauseate walking,' said she. ''Tis a country diversion. I loathe the country.' To Sir Wilfull Witwoud, also in *The Way of the World*, this thought occurred in his cups.

> Your Turks are infidels, and believe not in the grape. Your Mahometan, your Mussulman, is a dry stinkard – no offence, aunt. My map says that your Turk is not so honest a man as your Christian. I cannot find by the map that your Mufti is orthodox – whereby it is a plain case, that orthodox is a hard word, aunt and (*Hiccups*) Greek for claret. –
>
> To drink is a Christian diversion,
> Unknown to the Turk or the Persian:
> Let Mahometan fools
> Live by heathenish rules,
> And be damned over tea-cups and coffee.
> But let British lads sing,
> Crown a health to the king,
> And a fig for your sultan and sophy!

The diversion, as applied to road-ways and traffic, is a nuisance; this we all learned during the war when it became a synonym for a bomb-hole in the road which caused traffic to be turned aside. But social life without some straying would be dull indeed. We need the 'rale divert'.

DOD AND DODDLED

DODDLE is sometimes a form of dawdle, but it can also be applied to activity. I have been shown its use in letters about a century old as a variant for bothered. 'I really cannot be doddled to do it.' 'You had better go and get dodded', is, or was, the North Country suggestion of a hair-cut. And perhaps the answer was 'I can't be doddled'. Trees when lopped were dodded and became doddards. The use of Dod or Dodd for a bare summit like a shaven skull is familiar to lovers of the Lake District. It is exactly similar to the use of maol, which signifies a bald mountain in the Highlands of Scotland. The great Glas Maol which you pass on the way to Braemar from the south would be Green Dodd in Cumberland.

Doddypoll means a blockhead rather than a bald head. It sounds a friendly word. Such a fool would be one of Shakespeare's 'allowed fools' whose motley was a licence to jest with more or less impunity.

ENAMEL

'THE same, enamelled.' We do not take much notice of it in the Store's catalogue. But it was once a word of grace. Before it was associated with kitchenware and while it was a 'semi-opaque variety of glass, applied by fusion to metallic surfaces', poetry appreciated amel or the later enamel to signify richness of surface colouring. Marvell reminds the emigrants in Bermuda of God's bounty in melons, oranges and pomegranates. In the hues of the islands and 'the Mexique Bay'

> He gave us this eternal spring
> Which here enamels everything.

In *Lycidas* flowers are

> quaint enamelled eyes
> That on the green turf suck the honeyed showers.

In *The Two Gentlemen of Verona* there is not much of Shakespeare's early best, but at least one exquisite riverside note, and there enamel shines.

> The current that with gentle murmur glides,
> Thou knowst, being stopp'd, impatiently doth rage,
> But when his fair course is not hindered
> He makes sweet music with the enamelled stones,
> Giving a kiss to every gentle sedge
> He overtaketh in his pilgrimage.

Enamelled stones are more easily seen and their water-music more easily heard in mountain becks and burns than in midland or lowland streams with 'gentle sedge', but the enamel adds to the affection and admiration in the lines because of the (probably unconscious) play on words which the letters of love, 'am', bring in.

EVERLASTING

LISTENING to a superb performance of *Romeo and Juliet* I was struck by the excellent use which Shakespeare twice made of everlasting in this 'basketful of words'. The first occasion is when Friar Laurence, visited by the young pair seeking a swift marriage, breaks into poetry as exquisite as any spoken by the lovers themselves.

> Here comes the lady: O so light a foot
> Will ne'er wear out the everlasting flint.
> A lover may bestride the gossamer
> That idles in the wanton summer air
> And yet not fall: so light is vanity.

The roll of everlasting, a simple word yet poignant with the weight of years, is so happily contrasted with the slightness of gossamer. It gives sonority and substance to the lyrical music of the lines.

Then again Romeo dies with the same word fresh upon his lips.

O here
Will I set up my everlasting rest
And shake the yoke of inauspicious stars
From this world-wearied flesh.

There is profound valediction in everlasting.

The frenzied Timon, dwindling to his rest, knew it.

Come not to me again: but say to Athens,
Timon hath made his everlasting mansion
Upon the beachéd verge of the salt flood,
Who once a day with his embosséd froth
The turbulent surge shall cover: thither come
And let my grave-stone be your oracle.

Here, as so often, the letter 'r' is dominant and beats its drums of grief. In 'ever' it powerfully drives at the heart, whether it be in everlasting flints, rests, or mansions.

Others have had the impulse for the 'r' and for everlasting, and with no less effect. The famous passage from Traherne proclaims his ear for these.

> The corn was orient and immortal wheat, which never should be reaped nor ever was sown. I had thought it stood from everlasting to everlasting.

I am not sure about everlastingness.

But felt through all this fleshly dress
Bright shoots of everlastingness.

The 'ness' in some way weakens it.

Vaughan is happier with Eternity.

And in those weaker glories spy
Some shadows of eternity.

When I praise everlasting I am not forgetting the majesty of eternal.

EYEABLE

I HAVE been requested to shudder at eyeable as a synonym for worth looking at. But, if we have palatable for things eatable and drinkable which are worth tasting, there is no logical reason for dismissing eyeable or even noseable for charming ladies or delicious scents. 'Easy on the eye' is common usage for the former and I would as soon have eyeable as that. It can, however, be reasonably objected that eyeable is an ugly sound and thus bears hardly on the beauty suggested.

I am told that 'Clergyable' is the telegraphic address of a firm of ecclesiastical outfitters. It could serve as an alternative to marriageable; but, in these days of civil and secular weddings, we should then have to admit registrable too. To describe a spinster as clergyable but not very eyeable would reduce my correspondent on this subject to a fainting collapse, from which he could not, I think, be rescued by the old stimulant of noseable salts.

FROUNCE

THE 'l' of flounce has supervened upon an 'r'. There is something to be said for the old frounce which meant a wrinkle, a fold, a flounce, a deceit and a piece of titivation.

> Thus, Night, oft see me in thy pale career
> Till civil-suited Morn appear,
> Not tricked and frounced as she was wont
> With the Attic Boy to hunt,
> But kercheft in a comely cloud. . . .

Then there is the frowning frounce, caused by wrinkling or folding of brows. So a stern father could frounce in one sense upon a daughter too much frounced in the other.

FUMISH

HALL, the Tudor Chronicler who was one of Shakespeare's sources, wrote a full and lusty style and his adjectives are rich. The wickedness of the Yorkist aggressors is always hammered home with the adjective 'facinorous'. A strong Lancastrian and supporter of a strong monarchy, as a Tudor historian was wise to be, Hall was apt to dismiss rebels with a sharp crack of the pen. Of some resisters to the dominion of Henry IV he wrote, when they were reduced to panic, 'So much was their courage abated and their fumish crakes refrigerat with the remembraunce of their last conflicte and batail.' Fumish means, of course, smoky: but since there is no smoke without fire, it also implies anger and contumacity. Fumish is good for the description of a saucy, choleric mood that asks for refrigeration. Crake appears to be a boast or a brag as well as the harsh, grating cry which gave its name to the Corncrake. Fumish crakes together suggest the nastiest kind of utterance on the lips of 'facinorous and unmeasurable' (guilty and unrestrainable) wantons. Incidentally, I note that in Hall Richard II was called not only wanton, but unwitty, meaning unwise. Wit and wisdom had not then parted company.

GEW-GAW

TENNYSON in 'Maud' has

> Seeing his gew-gaw castle
> New as his title, built last year.

The Highlands of Scotland became an unhappy receptacle of gew-gaw 'places' – or palaces – when the wealth of that country's industrial centre coincided with a taste for modernized Baronial architecture and when the ship-builders became the holiday monarchs of the glen. With ample funds to encastle themselves, they left not a turret unraised in order to display their romanticism as well as their riches. I remember as a boy being taken by an intending purchaser to see a gruesome specimen of this kind, a monster in red sand-stone whose creator had carved over the door 'Except the Lord build the house their labour is but lost that build it.' The Suffragettes put an end to his plans for housing himself in Chieftain's style by burning the place down, a neat comment on the chosen text. Deity was thus exonerated. The gew-gaw castle evidently did not arise by heaven's command.

It is a fascinating word, this gew-gaw, especially in its earliest spelling of guy-gaw or gu-gaw. It has been applied to so many things from crowns (Dryden) to the odious contents of Ye Olde Gifte Shoppe. Scotland – as a Scot I must confess and curse the fact – has been an assiduous salesman of the gew-gaw. The shop at the beauty-spot where the motor coaches unload has always its blaze of toys, trinkets, and nick-nacks embellished – hateful word, but surely right in this connection – with tartans, authentic and otherwise. The midget bag-pipes jostle the bedizened hand-bags and photo-frames, usually proclaimed as 'Gifties frae yont the Border'. I believe that a lot of this junk is not made in Scotland and that some of it used to come from the Continent. But that does not palliate the offence of selling it. It can be urged that the tourist loves it: at any rate he accepts it. But I doubt if he would miss it if it was not there and 'gifties' of more style and dignity were in the shop-window instead. However that may be, the dismissive syllables of gew-gaw sum up this merchandise.

GESTIC

ACTORS and dancers may gesticulate, but our critics do not salute them for their gestic skill. There is a curious passage in Goldsmith's 'The Traveller' in which the author, discussing 'the bright domain' of France, observes

> How often have I led the sportive choir
> With tuneless pipe, beside the murmuring Loire!

Though, he says, his harsh touch faltered in the piping and 'mocked all tune',

> Yet would the village praise my wondrous power
> And dance, forgetful of the noon-tide hour.
> Alike all ages. Dames of ancient days
> Have led their children through the mirthful maze,
> And the gay grandsire, skill'd in gestic lore,
> Has frisk'd beneath the burden of threescore.

It is a startling picture and by no means complimentary to France, 'gay sprightly land of mirth and social ease', since its people are apparently described as tone-deaf and far from critical. However, there is an ample courtesy and hospitality to strangers in the conduct of the frisky and gestic grandfathers and of the dames unstiffened by longevity.

But was it so kindly an act of the Traveller to pipe when he couldn't?

GLOBAL

'THAT man's the best cosmopolite who loves his country best.' Must we now substitute globalist for cosmopolite? Certainly the adjective global is enjoying a large popularity. Some cannot bear the sight of it. But I do not see why the 'great globe itself' should not have an adjective and, if global is used to mean 'all round or all over the world', as in 'global war', I deny that any linguistic crime has been committed. What is senseless is the use of global to mean whole. I cannot think why the simple words whole and total have become so much disliked that over-all and global must be set in their places. Over-all is properly applicable to something that over-rides or stands over all else, e.g. a sovereign government. But it is ridiculous to talk of a man's over-all earnings when we mean only to describe his total income: it is equally absurd to speak of a team's over-all score in a game when all that is meant is the whole score of one side which might well be under the score of the other side.

V. H. Collins, in his excellent book on *The Choice of Words*, wherein he considers especially the employment of synonyms, quotes a splendid example of global thus misused. He found that a conference of doctors, passing a resolution upon negotiations between their own profession and the Ministry of Health, called upon the Minister 'to state what global sum should in his opinion be in the central pool to implement the recommendations of the Spens Report'. The motion could be translated thus. 'To state what total sum he thinks should be kept in the central pool to carry out the Spens Report.'

Mr. Collins uses the term show-word for the longer or more learned term which is preferred to the short and simple, e.g. commence instead of begin, and terminate instead of end. 'Global war' is not cumbrous and does not offend me by pomposity, but does it say more than 'world war'? On the other hand I think we ought not to be too suspicious or contemptuous of the longer word. The language does need variety and if we have nothing but end and begin, we may find our speech and writing becoming jejune. An exhibitionist's display of learning and piling up of syllables is irritating, of course, but there is room for an ample as well as a bare style. Would Mr. Collins have a modern Gibbon, should such arise, mend his ways and starve his sentences? Surely the speech and writing of Mr. Winston Churchill on matters fairly called global can be our guide here. Nobody can better employ the monosyllable when it suits his theme, or more richly roll out the sounding period when his subject invites this amplitude.

GLOUT

To glower at or frown. It is good, too, in its adjectival form, e.g. glouty weather, which is used in some parts of the country as an alternative to dowly. Owing to its resemblance to glue, glouty also suggests to me thick mud and stolchy, slutchy paths. But properly it belongs to the world of gloomy looks and threatening clouds. Gloom, which has remained inspissated to the cliché-lover since Dr. Johnson first called it that, is so apt to its own darkness that glouty seems weak beside it. The participle glouting appears in Garth's poem 'The Dispensary'.

> Glouting with sullen spite the fury shook
> Her clotted locks and blasted with each look.

Glout will not do for the encircling gloom of the hymn or for Tennyson's 'thousand years of gloom'. But it might be kept in conversational English. 'Don't glout at me, child' sums up the petulance of the spoiled. Gloom is for the more profound frustrations.

GREMIAL

A GREMIAL was a resident of a University, since he laid his learned head on the kindly breast or welcoming lap of that foundation. The Latin *gremium* for bosom or lap has given us also gremial for a bishop's silken apron, but I like the word best as an adjective for one who 'lives in'. In the old days of the drapery trade the housed assistants such as Art Kipps and Mr. Polly were not called gremials, I suppose, because their employers were rarely classical scholars. But gremials they were, though the bosom was apt to be flinty. Surely luxury, so frequently equipped with a lap by those who have a conservative taste in metaphor, should have its pampered gremials?

I came across gremial because I was investigating the existence of a verb, greminate. It does not, apparently, exist except by accident. One employed in the Horticultural Press had complained to me that germinate would keep on appearing on the rough proof as greminate. I therefore hoped that such a verb had some dictionary status. My gardening journalist believes that gremination, whether or no the lexicographers admit its presence, is perfectly suited to the high-pitched, whining species of complaint, the kind of noise, I would add, frequently made on the loftier reaches of the B.B.C. programmes by literary law-givers in a disparaging temper. Yes, I like gremination: it has the right moan of the outraged aesthete and of the petulant critics who are the gremials of the more exalted reviews.

GUARDIAN

THE *Manchester Guardian*, and all other papers and magazines which have had Guardian in their title, are fortunate. It was prudent of the founders to select a word so firm, so reassuring, and so comfortable (in the old strengthening sense of that fine adjective). The Army has rightly kept Guards for its most esteemed regiments. A poet can bring guard into a line with a certainty of sonorous power.

> Where the great vision of the guarded mount
> Looks towards Namancos and Bayona's hold.

Milton could make magic of geography and in this case the guarded mount strikes a proper chord for the roll of names to follow. An Angel sounds doubly protective if he is also a Guardian Angel. It is true that the Boards of Guardians won, here and there, some ill repute in our social history and so have vanished from the organization of the Welfare State. One can only say that they failed to live up to a name which should have inspired them to conduct which was noble, chivalrous and benign.

The title of 'Guardian' must surely be an asset to a publication. It is easy and agreeable to say: it suggests that the paper is a friend as well as a messenger. *Times* is convenient, but seems to offer the news of an epoch rather than of the day or the minute. *Express* and *Telegraph* have the right air of speed, while *Mail* has a leisurely sound, as though all its news came in by post. It is queer that when the young Harmsworth was founding the new model of on-the-spot and bustling popular journalism, always striving to be first with the news and most forthright with the views, he should have selected *Mail* rather than something more volatile or flamboyant. *News* is a simple statement, but *News Chronicle* is repetitive, based on an amalgamation, and so hardly an asset at the paper-stall. *Manchester Guardian* is certainly a mouthful, but in Lancashire, and perhaps elsewhere, too, a demand for *Guardian* will produce the right result. *Observer* is rather a chilly name and suggests judicious detachment while *Guardian* is warmly proclaiming its zeal on your behalf. *Argus* is too classical and *Standard* is somewhat regal and medieval. *Star* is good for illumination of the evening. One that fascinates me is the *Surrey Comet*, all speed and blaze. But for solid and consoling worth, *Guardian* leads the titular field.

HELLION

'I'M given to explosive rages,' wrote Tallulah Bankhead in an autobiography whose chatty prose seemed to gurgle like her voice. 'Three or four times a day I'm irritated to the point I want to commit murder. Shrinking from the penalty, I fall back on my tongue. I'm something of a hellion when I lash out.'

What exactly is a hellion? The *Oxford English Dictionary* has not heard of the creature. Hell cats, or in Scotland hellicats, are on the register of the wayward at best and the fiendish at worst. Another good hell-word is hell-bender. This is the American salamander, listed as 'a repulsive amphibian' or 'a protracted and reckless debauch'. A hellion going hell-bent or hell-for-leather on a hell-bender would touch the limits of infernality.

The mythical salamander was a lizard apparently made of asbestos and immune from the effects of cookery. He has given us the powerful salamandrine, applicable to those who can stand up to any roasting criticism. Miss Bankhead, the self-styled hellion, demands occasionally a salamandrine quality in those whom she describes with her pen. But she is not a flame-thrower with only an outward target and is quite ready to scorch herself with self-criticism.

HEN

NOT long ago I wrote an article on the then (and perhaps still) prevalent and friendly habit of calling unknown people 'ducks' and of saying 'love' at first sight, e.g. 'Hold tight, love' or 'Here's your change, ducks', as shouted by the London bus-conductress to her passengers, male or female. I suggested that the men might at least be 'drakey, dear' instead of being lumped with the ducks. It was then pointed out to me, by a correspondent in Glasgow, that on the public transport vehicles of that city I would find myself addressed as Hen. Is this yet another reference to human beings as the poultry of the Welfare State? Or is it a corruption and abbreviation of hinny, which is itself a corruption of honey? Have the hinnies of the Northern English counties crossed the border and become the hens of Glasgow?

The equalitarian practices of our time have made a queer muddle of our forms of greeting. A barrow-boy may greet my wife with a 'Nahce bananas, lidy!' which is almost reverent, or he may cry 'Nahce bananas, ducks!' which is not. Me he will probably call 'Guv' and to be a Governor is to be an Excellency; this is high compliment indeed. The good lady who kept my 'local' fifteen years ago used to greet her selected customers of the Saloon Bar with 'Good evening, Squire'. To be in the squirearchy does not, in fact, imply such high social station as a Governorship, but Governor did fall a trifle when it was the fashion for schoolboys to call their fathers by this name, a habit which *O.E.D.* marks as beginning in 1827.

Another form which the barrow-boy may use to me is 'cock'. Well, that is better than the 'hen' which I am promised in Glasgow.

Darling, as used between those who hardly know each other and almost certainly dislike each other, is used in England mainly by Bohemians and 'theatrical parties'. But I am told of a 'daily help' who, on leaving her employer, always says, 'Ta-ta, madam, darling'. Perhaps my bus-conductress will soon be greeting me with a 'Hold tight, Squire Ducks'. Or 'Hold Very Tight'. Why, I wonder, do the London Transport workers love to be so emphatic? I would have thought that 'Hold Tight' was a sufficient warning of a jerky start to come, but the usual form is 'Hold Very Tight There'. As it is the habit to slur the first word and stress what follows, I am continually hearing 'Very tight, there' shouted at passengers who seem to be perfectly sober.

HOG'S NORTON

MR. GILLIE POTTER, in his amusing discourse on the stage or at the microphone, has used Hog's Norton as a typical English village-name. His Hog's Nortonian family of decayed squires became known to all. Then it was pointed out that there actually is such a hamlet. Furthermore I learn, from reading the life of Beau Nash of Bath, that the name was used in the eighteenth century to be a symbol of crude rusticity. Nash, as arbiter of elegance and master of polite ceremonies, was trying to dissuade or prevent the local squires from coming into the routs and revels in their riding-boots. He had to bring ridicule to the aid of ordinance and did so by composing 'Frontinella's Invitation to the Assembly'.

> Come, one and all, to Hoyden Hall,
>   For there's the assembly this night;
>   None but prude fools,
>   Mind manners and rules;
> We Hoydens do decency slight.
>
>   Come, Trollops and Slatterns,
>   Cockt hats and white aprons,
> This best our modesty suits;
>   For why should not we
>   In dress be as free
> As Hog's-Norton squires in boots?

It does not seem to me a very powerful attack on the Tony Lumpkins whose natural hebetude would render them invulnerable against verbal satire. But Nash backed this with a puppet-show in which Punch was shown going to bed in his boots and spurs and finally driven off the stage by his spur-galled mistress. When further he told a lout who came booted to the Assembly that he had forgotten his horse, victory over Hog's Norton was complete.

HONORARIUM

MOST people do not object to receiving money: honourable men need not boggle about the name of the reward, if it be honestly earned. Whether their cheque or packet be dubbed pay, salary, or even the dibs or the doings, they value it by the source and the content, not the label. To be salary-earning, instead of wage-earning, may imply slightly more security because longer 'notice' of discharge may be attached to the salary. But, in essence, they are *quid pro quo*. And what is wrong with that?

But there are still some who appear to be touchy about receiving money at all, even for good work well done. The Secretary of a Club, for example, often receives nothing so common as a salary: he is presented with an Honorarium. This permits him to write Honorary in front of Secretary, which I take to be nonsense. The man is paid, and rightly paid, for the work which he does to the Club's satisfaction. So why should he shamefacedly pretend to be an amateur? For the sake of Honorarium-addicts I hope that the Income Tax Assessors regard this recompense as fairy gold, an accidental gift, and so untaxable. But I can hardly believe that such clemency exists in a tribe in whom the quality of mercy is, to put it mildly, somewhat strained.

An Honorarium is, according to the informative Mr. V. H. Collins, 'a voluntary payment for professional services'. I do not understand the relevance of 'voluntary'. All salaries are voluntarily paid by the employer: the Club is not forced to use this particular Secretary. The emphasis is surely on the word professional, and there is no shame attached to knowing one's job and carrying it out for money. To ears distressed by any mention of money matters, Honorarium is an escape-word and so smacks of humbug. It may sound fine; but so do fiddle-sticks, properly handled.

It has long been the habit of the genteel to use these escape-words. Why should the parson have a stipend instead of a salary or even, to use the common slang, a 'screw'? The same word has been attached in Britain to full-time magistrates; they are known as stipendiaries. But the fact is that they are experienced professionals drawing their appointed salaries. At what stage does a tip become a bonus or a gratuity? And when is a fee an emolument? This last seems to me the most pretentious of all the escape-words. If my writings yield me the 'boodle', the money in the bank, that satisfies me. I want no emoluments.

HOWFF

THE Scots have prudently kept alive the word howff for a place of resort, a haunt and a rendez-vous. It is more cosy and confidential than the current English term, 'the local'. It is as old as Allan Ramsay's cordial Edinburgh of the early eighteenth century and Ramsay was a voluble mourner of vanished howff-wives such as bawdy Lucky Spence or Maggy Johnston. The latter's repute was more respectable, her trade being not in bad company but in good ale, 'very white, clear, and intoxicating' – of which she sold the Scots Pint, which is near Two Quarts English, for twopence! Her establishment was the Nineteenth Hole of the Bruntsfield Links.

> Whan we were weary'd at the Gowff,
> Then Maggy Johnston's was our Howff;
> Now a' our Gamesters may sit dowff,
>   Wi' Hearts like Lead,
> Death wi' his Rung rax'd her a Yowff,
>   And sae she died.

Dowff is mournful, Rung a heavy staff, and Yowff a swinging blow. Since I have already commented on the various meanings of the word bang, it may be worth mentioning in addition that Maggie's much-frequented howff was described by Ramsay as having a bang of patrons, i.e. a good quantity. But a casual customer could not talk of such a place as his howff: that would imply the intimacy of regular support. In Scotland a kindly host will still mention to his intended guest that such-and-such a club or tavern is the howff where he is likely to be found.

HURDY-GURDY

It is odd to think that the hurdy-gurdy began as a lute-like instrument, whose strings are sounded by the revolution of a rosined wheel. To me the noisy-sounding double-barrelled name seems exactly right for the raucous, jovial barrel-organ which is now so rarely a disturber of the peace or a stimulant of free-and-easy dancing in the street. Towards the close of the last century the House of Commons considered hurdy-gurdies gravely, setting them time limits for their services, morning and evening. The night was to be kept inviolate from the sacred music of Calverley's

> Grinder who serenely grindest
> At my door the Hundredth Psalm,
> Till thou ultimately findest
> Pence in thy unwashen palm.

J. K. Stephen sprang to the defence of the grinder against this oppressive measure.

> When the dawn with rosy finger
> Dissipates the eastern gloom,
> You and your machine must linger
> Silent in your silent room.

The hurdy-gurdy achieved the honour of salutation by two of

England's past masters of light verse. But neither of them gave it that homely name.

INBIGGIT

I HAVE heard Scots talk of an inbiggit man, meaning one built in, egocentric, and so silent. A little book on the language of the Shetlanders defines it as 'morose, uncommunicative'. In England the inbiggit are now called introverts. But the Scottish word beats the Latin one. There is something more striking and picturesque in this suggestion of one who is his own fire-side with a protective covering of stone; none will touch the secret of him who has made such architecture of his isolation. He is not just thrawn (cross-grained) by chance of character. He has worked to preserve his private life and to keep his peace. Since biggins for buildings is (or was) common in the North of England, there is no reason why the inbiggit man should be only met north of the Border.

INDIGO

THE colour is dark and rich; the word is right for the tint and the menace. The tincture has a gloomy origin, for decomposing is not an adjective that attracts. Indigo 'is produced by the decomposition of the glucoside Indican, which exists also in woad'. A more hideous name for a colour than woad it is impossible to imagine. It has been a bitter misfortune of the Ancient Britons that their schemes of self-adornment, which may have been pleasant enough, should have been burdened with this nasty monosyllable. The Modern Britons, feminine, also paint themselves, but they ask for such romantically sounding articles as Mascara in order to achieve their ends. One cannot imagine the Bond Street specialist advertising their latest line in Woad or Madam demanding anything so offensive to the ear.

But Indigo, employed to describe the blue-violet colour of an evening sky or of far-off mountains, is handsome enough to figure in a lyric such as Arthur Symons used to write of the ballet scene and its hues.

> Lights in a coloured mist
> From indigo to amethyst.

It is strange that ballet has not evoked more poetry in our time.

INEBRIATE

THERE is a certain solid splendour about inebriation. A Home for Inebriates sounds almost respectable. Amid the squalid modern terms for exaltation by the grape or the grain, the blottos, stinkos, plastereds and so on, the inebriate stands like a gentleman with vine-leaves in his hair. Let the stinkos stagger and the blottos lurch. Inebriation has the dignified tread of one who knows that he must, despite all cause and inclination to sway, put up a seemly show of unwavering progress. As for the uninebriating cup of tea, most people attribute the notion of its sober virtue to William Cowper.

> And while the bubbling and loud hissing urn
> Throws up a steamy column and the cups,
> That cheer but not inebriate, wait on each,
> So let us welcome peaceful evening in!

But Cowper was borrowing. The idealist philosopher George Berkeley, so crudely refuted by Dr. Johnson in the matter of objective reality, had already applied the phrase to tar-water, whose virtues he strongly proclaimed. He described this fluid as being 'of a nature so mild and benign and proportioned to the human constitution as to warm without heating, to cheer but not inebriate'.

Disraeli's description of Gladstone as 'a sophistical rhetorician, inebriated with his own verbosity' is, incidentally, a pretty piece of involved alliteration. Note the pattern of the 's's, 'r's, and 'b's. The weight of inebriated, matching verbosity, is necessary to the sentence. 'Drunk with his own garrulity' would never have been remembered as a direct hit upon the political wind-bag, which Disraeli, justly or unjustly, associated with his rival.

A charming reference to uninebriation occurs in a poem on Milk by 'Gentleman Jerningham' – and how genteel that eighteenth-century dramatist and minor poet could be! He felt deeply on the subject of Wet Nursing and those who

> To venal hands the smiling babe consign
> While Hymen starts and Nature drops a tear.

How much more praiseworthy are the nursing mothers.

> For you, ye plighted fair, when Hymen crowns
> With tender offspring your unshaken love,
> Behold them not with Rigour's chilling frowns,
> Nor from your sight unfeelingly remove.
>
> Unsway'd by Fashion's dull unseemly jest,
> Still to the bosom let your infant cling,
> There banquet oft, an ever-welcome guest,
> Unblam'd inebriate at that healthful spring.

What better praise of that gremial Shrine, as Jerningham so movingly described it, 'where Nature with presaging aim . . . The snowy nectar pours, delightful streams!'?

JOSKIN

'I HATE the joskins', wrote Charles Lamb. Thus he dismissed the rustics, which was silly as well as uncharitable. It is curious that the intellectual snobbery of townees should have touched even that amiable spirit. It has always astonished me that the 'cits' should be so confident of their own superiority and regard the human fauna of the farmlands as block-headed bumpkins. Later on, with reference to the term pagan, I call attention to the overweening pride of the townsfolk who used, with a bitter contempt, this word which simply meant villager, to disparage, with a suggestion of vicious barbarism, all not of their own religious creed. Such conduct is quite in tune with the urban arrogance which has continually insulted the man who by his work in the fields feeds his fellow in the office and the factory.

Bumpkins and hayseeds, clod-polls and clod-hoppers, joskins and turnip-heads – that has been the reward of the ploughing and the harvest, the milk and meat. Yet the general farm labourer, who may be called unskilled because he has no special department, is in fact skilled in a number of difficult as well as laborious crafts. He has to use his wits as well as his hands and, at least within my experience, the joskin shows at least as much common sense in discussing general topics as any city worker. Because he is less oppressed by print, he is less subject to be overwhelmed by slogans and catchwords.

I do not advocate a neo-Wordsworthian cult of St. Joskin on the ground that

> An impulse from the vernal wood
> Can teach us more of man,
> Of moral evil and of good
> Than all the sages can.

The hayseed does not become Socratic merely by close acquaintance with sheep. On the other hand he is not necessarily a bad judge of ideas because he is a good judge of a ram or a bull. But all these joskin and bumpkin taunts grow rapidly out of date. For he who goes to mow a meadow is now a skilled mechanic and the best man of the soil is he who can soonest repair a tractor that has broken down. Cold Comfort Farm is that which has run out of petrol and the supposed turnip-head turns out to be a technocrat.

JUJUBE

ASKED to comment on jujube, I reply that it is my least favourite sweet (liquorice excepted) and that it is not unfairly labelled with such a hideous name. (Sweetened and thickened into a Fruit Pastille the jujubish article can be soothing, but in its smooth, half-transparent form it is no better than a cough drop.) The name suggests African jungles to me: so I was astonished to discover that the jujube is an Ancient Greek, being a corruption of zizyphon, 'an edible berry like drupe', the latter being 'a pulpy fruit with a nutty kernel'. Hence a gelatinous sweet of somewhat the same shape became a zizyphon and later a jujube. *O.E.D.* mentions 'The Lotus Eaters, whose favourite fruit still grows under the name of the jujube on the same coast'.

Tennyson, lyricist of Lotus-eating, appears to have missed something here. He might have written,

> The Jujube blooms below the barren peak:
> The Jujube blows by every winding creek:
> All day the wind breathes low with mellower tone;
> Through every hollow cave and alley lone,
> Round and round the spicy down the yellow jujube-dust is blown.

He could also have ended with

> Oh rest, ye brother mariners, we will not wander more
> But jubilate for ever on this Jujubaceous shore.

But he remained loyal to Lotus.

The names of sweets are sometimes oddly gloomy. Lozenge, for example, the jujube's cousin, originally meant a tombstone, being a slab of the burial kind. It then became a rhomb or a diamond-shape. Next it was something of that form small enough to be dissolved in the mouth. Now we have abundance of throat-lozenges which seek to save us from coughing our way into the ancient lozenge that was lapidary and sepulchral.

KIBOSH

THE dictionary gives it as Yiddish. At the beginning of the 1914 war there was a music-hall song whose chorus announced

> Belgium put the kibosh on the Kaiser,
> Serbia took a stick and rammed it home.

This statement was, in 1914, more optimistic than accurate and, in view of the facts, the ditty was soon abandoned. But kiboshing is such a thwacking word that it will be long with us.

I was surprised that it was in use in Dickens's London. But the spelling was different. In Boz's paper on Seven Dials, street-fighting is described as a frequent and not ungenial occurrence. He watches some indignation boil up over the use of the word hussies, then, apparently, much more offensive than now. (Our vigour of feminine abuse has intensified.) The objection to the term is sustained by an interloper 'who has evinced a strong inclination throughout to get up a branch fight on her own account. "Hooroar", ejaculates a pot-boy, "put the kye-bosk on her, Mary!"'

LABORIOUS

WHEN did laborious begin to lose its quality of commendation and to acquire the meaning of heavy and tedious? The Rev. John Prince in *The Worthies of Devon* (1701), wrote of a 'laborious and prudent pastor' and, in so doing, he implied the conscientious servant of the parish and careful maker of a sermon and not the dreary effort of a bore. But Milton had already given the adjective a tincture of unpleasantness and contrasted it with happier states.

> I will point ye out the right path of a virtuous and noble Education; laborious indeed at the first ascent, but else so smooth, so green, so full of goodly prospect and melodious sounds on every side that the harp of Orpheus was not more charming.

Prince also used painful in its earliest and natural sense, suffering pain. He wrote of 'a painful clergyman' not to suggest that the poor man was a public nuisance but that he was a private sufferer.

It is odd that the pain in painful is now so often something inflicted and not the condition of which the sufferer is full. A scratch can still be painful to its recipient. But the performance of an artist is, when called painful, a torture only to others: he probably enjoyed it himself. This reminds me of a little girl's sensible way of expressing her desire to 'come in for dessert'. 'Mother,' she said, 'I do feel fruitless.'

LAY-BY

I AM so often critical of officials and officialese that it is pleasant to find cause for praise. Might we not congratulate those local authorities who not only set aside road-side resting-places for the weary driver but call them by this simple, pleasant name of lay-by? One would have expected some much more formidable title. 'Site scheduled for parking adjacent to highway two hundred yards forward.' Lay-by says it all in two cosy syllables. The term, I believe, was first used on rivers and canals for reaches of water where barges could be moored without hindering the traffic, and it was a good idea to transfer it to the roads. Lay-by has a lullaby sound and invites to a merited snooze. The driver of a heavy vehicle who has been long at the wheel and has another long spell to come is well advised to take his siesta in a lay-by where he causes nobody to swing out in order to pass him.

LAZY-BED

GEORGE SCOTT-MONCRIEFF, in his book on *The Scottish Islands*, writes of Harris: 'Cultivation is done in lazy-beds. Where the name lazy-bed came from, goodness knows: it is no lazy job to fill these scraps of soil between rocks, on the edge of bogs and ditches, overhanging the sea. Shape and size dictated by the exigencies of the terrain, the lazy-beds form low humps, rather like the upturned grass over a new grave and often no bigger, comprised of the poor earth enriched with dung and seaweed, growing potatoes or oats, flaunting green among the barren stones.' Elsewhere too among the bony islands, the Hebridean skeleton, so grey and gaunt today, so blue and silvery tomorrow, he notes these patches torn from infertility by prolonged and patient labour. Lazy-beds indeed! Unless the term is a corruption of some Gaelic word, the Hebrideans have a mordant sense of humour.

But lazy-beds are not in the islands only. Potato-growers elsewhere have used the term. But I can find no explanation of the name, except in the sour jest of a man afflicted with a back-ache and suffering sore labour's lumbago.

LEAFING

A CORRESPONDENT with a grievance has written to tell me that he has been 'leafing' my last book; he would not, of course, admit that he had disgraced himself by actually reading the contemptible object. He had, no doubt with a sniff and a slight shudder, just gone so far as to turn the leaves. This used to be called skipping or thumbing. But I am grateful for leafing; it is an accurate term for casual or disdainful turning of the pages.

It reminds me of that superb aloofness suggested in the commonly used phrase 'My attention has been drawn'. The words are familiar to journalists. When somebody believes that a statement in your paper is libellous and actionable – or has been wheedled into thinking so by a third-rate solicitor hungry for work and fees – he can hardly bring himself to admit that he reads, or even leafs, your odious and contemptible rag. Accordingly he informs you that his attention has been drawn, etc. etc. Who drew it? Was it the solicitor or a helpful friend? Or is there a profession of Attention Drawers who pore over the day's Press, find something they believe to be a possible course of action and source of damages, and then ring up the victim? 'I don't know, Sir, whether you chanced to notice the monstrous statement about you in the *Daily Verity*? I presume that a gentleman in your position would not subscribe to an organ of that character. So I thought I would draw your attention . . .' Leafers, like those whose attention has thus to be drawn, can sit back uncontaminated by what has been written. They do not disgrace themselves by doing more than glance at what others, with lower standards, actually read. I am grateful to my pained correspondent; at least I have done more than leaf his letter.

The opposite of leafing is, I think, perlustration, which means travelling throughout and carefully examining a territory; it is transferred to the careful scanning of books. I now await a letter from a more genial correspondent who will assure me that he perlustrates every word that comes from my pen.

LEMONADE

WHILE no great devotee of lemonade I cannot deny the beauty of its look and sound upon a printed page. I think of it when I read that the Crystal Palace is to rise from its ruins and its ashes and once more to be a pleasure-ground and possibly a centre of instruction. For to C. S. Calverley this was a Victorian picnic haunt where

> maidens crunch
> The sounding celery-stick or ram
> The knife into the blushing ham.

Above all, it was the home of soft drinks and the tender passion.

> Such are the sylvan scenes that thrill
> This heart! The lawns, the happy shade,
> Where matrons, whom the sunbeams grill,
> Stir with slow spoon their lemonade:
> And maidens flirt (no extra charge)
> In comfort at the fountain's marge!

John Betjeman, too, in 'Archaeological Picnic' cries

> Drink, Mary, drink your fizzy lemonade.

He bids the elders make their ecclesiastical and architectural research among

> Sweet smell of cerements and cold wet stones,
> Hassock and cassock, paraffin and pew.

But for the children let there be relief from scholarship and a slaking of thirst.

> For you, where meadow-grass is evidence,
> With flattened pattern, of our picnic made,
> One bottle more of fizzy lemonade!

The word chimes: the poet might be referring to a noble vintage for consumption with a serenade.

How different is ginger beer! One cannot feel lyrical on hearing of such 'pop'. Accurately Betjeman has likened it to the foam of the seas on a Cornish shore.

> But all that August those terrific waves
> Thundered defeat along the rocky coast
> And ginger-beery surf hissed 'Christabel'.

Such surf is frothy to the eye in the way of bottled 'minerals' and it does hiss, as Betjeman suggests. But, on a test of noise and looks, lemonade is my choice. Ginger-beer I set aside with Tizer and Cydrax. Lemonade can be effervescent or serene in any verbal company.

LILY-SILVERED

THE double word, which hyphenates noun and adjective, is common, but it can be very subtly used even when both the components are by no means strange. Those who regard Pope only as a master of rhymed epigram and rhetoric must be astonished to find – and they need not read long to find it – his magical and lyrical touch. It is especially manifest in his employment of these doubletons.

> To isles of fragrance, lily-silvered vales
> Diffusing languor in the panting gales;
> To lands of singing and of dancing slaves,
> Love-whisp'ring woods and lute-resounding waves.

Dr. Edith Sitwell notes 'the exquisite floating coolness of these lines'. The tribute is most just. Part of the music is the subtle alliteration, in which the letter 'l' runs with the liquid fascination of a purling stream. It is worth noting that while the adjectives and nouns employed to make the three doubletons in the four lines are familiar the linking of them produces an unfamiliar charm. Pope was often among the romantics, if we accept 'strangeness with beauty' as one of the definitions of romance.

Among the appalling horrors of *Titus Andronicus* are some exquisite lines which put Shakespeare's signature upon this early effort to give the groundlings a blood-pudding to their taste. 'Enter Lavinia, her hands cut off, and her tongue cut out, and ravisht.' Could ghastliness go further? Yet the beauty breaks in when Marcus Andronicus exclaims,

> O had the monster seen those lily hands
> Tremble, like aspen leaves, upon a lute.

I mention this because lily and lute, so frequent in any Elizabethan cluster of fair and fair-sounding things, are here in company, as they were in the lines of Pope already quoted.

We are more accustomed to lily-livered than to lily-silvered; white-livered is an old term, but the flowery variant lily-livered seems to have come in with the Victorians.

LONG

WHY do we long for things? Why did Cleopatra have 'immortal longings'? Can there be a derivation from, or at least a connection with, the old 'think long', which implied regret and desire as well as cogitation? I am reminded of that phrase as it occurs in the fifteenth century Paston Letters. 'I think right long to hear tidings', Margery Paston wrote. 'Sir, I pray you, if you tarry long at London, that it will please you to send for me, for I think long since I lay in your arms.' There is an easy transition, by abbreviation, from 'thinking right long' to longing for a loved one.

I have been sent an Ulster poem (author Richard Rowley) in which thinking long occurs in the last line of each sad stanza. I quote one of them.

> A poor oul' doitered man
> That yammers and girns,
> A was quarely different onst
> Wi' wife and bairns.
> The house was full o' weans
> All straight and strong;
> It's desprit lonely now
> An' A'm thinking long . . .

The loneliness of the old could hardly be described with a simpler power and pathos.

Why do we use 'So long' for adieu or goodbye? Is it linked with the conditional 'so long', which has come to mean little more than 'if'?

> So long as men can breathe, or eyes can see,
> So long lives this, and this gives life to thee.

We can imagine how so long as, first meaning while, was changed into a conditional phrase. This slang 'so long' of ours – so long as life remains or fortune favours? – has a kind of sad poetry within it. It is less optimistic than cheerioh, less devout than adieu, less confident than au revoir, less melancholy than farewell, which, for all its good intentions, does ring a solemn bell. Unite long and farewell and what a width and depth of parting is implied.

> Farewell, a long farewell, to all my greatness!

Now it is 'goodbye to all that' or even 'so long to the lot of it'.

LOUNGE AND GANGLE

I THINK that many people must wince when they see the word Lounge applied to a room or a suit of clothes. It is an ugly word and, as a rule, denotes an ugly posture. Even those who have to use it do not like it. I was reading the '*Monthly Bulletin* – a Magazine representing the determination inside and outside the brewing industry to improve public houses and to maintain an adequate licensing law' and had decided that no publication can ever have had a longer title to introduce a neater little dozen of well-written pages. Then I noted in the praise of a new inn, The Woolpack of King's Lynn: 'The lounge – that odious but now universally accepted word – is a room of distinction.' Not having been to King's Lynn, an error I consistently repent yet fail to correct, I cannot in this case assess the distinction. But I can strongly agree with the expression of odium.

I hate 'lounge-halls', so dear to descriptive house agents and scene-setting dramatists, since they are almost certain to be draughty. Lounge-halls suit the playwrights, especially the makers of farces, because places thus called can have more entrances and exits than are natural to an ordinary sitting-room and so are accommodating to guilty husbands caught with an excess of feminine company; but I do not, in real life, wish to sit amid an assortment of doors and staircases. I prefer a room. In inns let there be smoking-rooms, snugs and parlours. These there are sometimes; but increasingly there are the lounges. The lounge of an inn may be hideous in decoration or it may be handsome and done with taste; but the word disgusts me. As for the Grand Hotels, they must have names for their sitting-rooms. In that case I prefer even the Palm Court (with or without Palms) or the Winter Garden (with or without flowers) to the ubiquitous Lounge.

Why, by the way, are so many Hotel Lounges such factories of gloom? The clutter of Trade Journals, only there because they have been sent in free, the tiled fireplace of a sickly gamboge, the carpet selected because you can spill anything on it without noticeably staining it, and the chairs of varnished wickerwork are the ingredients, for me, of a melancholy beyond endurance. If their choice had been dictated by the local theatre and cinemas, they could not more efficiently compel me to get up and get out and do my sitting – I shall not say lounging – somewhere else, even if it means watching a third-rate 'second feature' amid the 'choc-ice' and Wurlitzer of a Palasseum. In the hotel I shall be worse bored, 'Lounjun' rown' en suffer'n,' as Uncle Remus said.

Yet lounge has a good enough origin in lungis, a medieval word for an awkward lout. To lounge is properly descriptive of this oaf in his repose. Sherlock Holmes's Dr. Watson observed of London that it was 'the great cesspool into which all the loungers of the Empire are drained'. This is unkind to London, but the linking of loungers with sewage shows a powerful distaste for the word lounge. I cannot see why a man's ordinary suit should be distinguished from his Sunday-go-to-meeting attire or his black coat and pin-stripe trousers by being called a lounge-suit. Myriads go to work in clothes thus stigmatized as proper to lollers and loafers. Those lounging at home usually do so in tweed coats and flannel trousers. I refuse to ask for a lounge-suit and merely suggest a suit, adding a further hint as to the colour in mind.

There is now a vogue for the adjective 'gangling'. When I first saw it I did not know what it meant. English dictionaries, too, do not know it. I suppose it is an American importation. It has certainly established itself in journalism and in the composition of popular fiction. There I am now continually meeting gangling fellows, but, since they may be busily engaged while all a-gangle, I take it to mean loose-limbed rather than lolling and lounging creatures. It is not a bad word: it creates a picture. Is there a verb to gangle for to sprawl about? Presumably there must be, since we use the participle. Why not also a noun? An up-to-date hotel might call the Lounge the Gangle. There would then be the double implication of ganging up and getting together as well as of loafing and sprawling.

Lounge has been used of towns as well as of rooms, though it may only have been Manservant's English. Fag, in the first scene of Sheridan's *The Rivals*, tells Thomas that Bath is 'a good lounge'.

LUBBER-FIEND

OUR modern Trade Unionists would have sour looks and doubtless some restrictive action for the lubber-fiend, the drudging Goblin of Milton, who

> sweat
> To earn his cream-bowl duly-set,
> When in one night, ere glimpse of morn
> His shadowy flail hath threshed the corn
> That ten day-labourers could not end.

The Russians, while their scientific materialism would be averse to goblins, would welcome such a Stakhanovite, as they call the man of exceptional production. It is hard to see why the creature of prodigious output should have lubber in his name, for a lubber was not only a clumsy oaf but an idler. And why a fiend as well as a loafer? However that may have happened, a lubber-fiend is the required home companion of many a mother and housekeeper today, since we are told that 'he performs some of the drudgery of the household during the night'. One can imagine the murmur of relief. 'Just leave all that washing-up beside the sink. It's the lubber-fiend's night in.' 'Fiend angelical!' as Juliet remarked of another matter.

He was also Lob-lolly and Lob-by-the-fire. Again there is the suggestion of a lazy lout, a gross injustice to this creature of kindly chores, the untiring scullion. The verb lob also connotes slow, dawdling, the tennis-ball hit high, the cricket-ball delivered underhand, and with more guile than pace. Cabs cruising for a fare go lobbing. It was unfair to call the busy and volatile Puck, who would nowadays be termed a global traveller at supersonic speed, the 'lob of spirits', unless the lob is here synonymous with the industrious, obliging lubber-fiend.

MALADJUSTED

THERE is always a taste for 'escape' words. In our swearing we slur over the sacred names and employ such evasions as Gosh and Cripes. The Greeks were so frightened of calling the Furies furious that they actually spoke of them as Eumenides, the Kindly Ones, the Well-Disposed, thinking thus to escape the attentions of these unpleasant creatures. The fashionable escapism of our time is to pretend that the old and simple words, bad and mad, are inapplicable to modern conduct. We must slide away from sin into maladjustment and from insanity into schizophrenia.

The danger about these escape words is that they are used so loosely. I recently attended a Medical Discussion Society and, in the course of some informal conversation, before the formal meeting, I discovered that the three doctors with whom I was talking did not agree at all about the meaning of schizophrenia. Divided mind – yes. But how far divided? One said that the word schizophrenia could only be applied to those with personalities so far split that they were violent and dangerous, while another applied it to minor eccentrics who were harmless.

In the case of ethics the bad boy or girl, usually disguised as a juvenile delinquent – another escape word – is commonly explained as being maladjusted. So that adjective has to appear in every article on the Young Offender. The general implication of these articles is that the State, i.e. the taxpayer, must kindly readjust the maladjusted. That, often, may be necessary. But there is another side to it which the articles usually omit. Surely the maladjusted might, under reasonable pressure, do quite a lot in the way of self-adjustment. We are all of us maladjusted to something and, if we have any character, we endeavour to put that right. I am myself wretchedly adjusted to the study and practice of mathematics. But, since it was necessary to reach a certain standard in this exhausting exercise if I was to continue with subjects to me more rewarding and enjoyable, I managed, with some groaning, to adjust my untrigonometrical brain and anti-logarithmic disposition to a sufficient mastery of these matters. None of my masters believed that I would be repressed or warped if I thus coped, under pressure, with mathematics. In short, I was curtly told to get a move on and adjust myself and I cannot believe that it did me any harm.

That was the common discipline of the time and place, and it may have been hard on a few who were so completely maladjusted to the curriculum that they could make no progress and derive no benefit at all. But the excuse of maladjustment has now been carried absurdly far in the other direction. Most of the supposedly maladjusted could pull themselves together if they were firmly handled, which does not mean brutally handled. However, as these notes are supposed to be verbal and not sociological, I shall drop the subject. But I shall continue to be considerably annoyed whenever I see the word maladjusted – also the word schizophrenia – dragged in as a mere cover for naughtiness or idleness or silliness, and without further definition of its meaning in each case.

MAWL

THE old English word for a hammer, spelled mawl, maul, or mall, is not commonly used now. But New York is more retentive. When Damon Runyon's Rusty Charley appears at Nathan Detroit's 'Crap

Game', 'the players are packed so close that you cannot get a needle between two guys with a mawl'. London has its Pall Mall still, but it has been flattened in common pronunciation into Pell Mell. (The word pell-mell, meaning confusedly, is derived from the French for medley and has nothing to do with hammering, although it is in pell-mell form that a hammered army may retire.) The Mall was the alley where the ball was struck or lifted with what we might now call a mallet. There is no more playing of Mall in central London, but the game survives here and there, one of its last refuges being in Hampstead, in the garden of the Freemasons' Arms at the bottom of Downshire Hill, not many yards from John Keats's house and garden in what is now Keats' Grove.

England has also forgotten another hammer-name, the beetle, except when it occurs in the old tavern-title, 'The Beetle and Wedge'. 'Fillip me with a three-man beetle,' said Sir John Falstaff, referring to the largest mawl of his time which needed the strength of three to swing it and represented for him the vast steam-hammer of our own mechanic age. The actor playing Sir John would not care to be filliped by a critic-beetle such as Mr. Ambrose Hammer, another of Damon Runyon's creations. 'He is what is called a dramatic critic by trade and his job is to write pieces for the paper about the new plays that someone is always producing on Broadway, and Ambrose's pieces are very interesting indeed, as he loves to heave the old harpoon into actors if they do not act to suit him, and as it will take a combination of Katharine Cornell, Jimmy Durante, and Lilian Gish to really suit Ambrose, he is generally harpooning away very good.'

No artist cares to be hammered with a mawl or mauled in the other sense of clawed and torn. It would be kinder to tap him with the critical mallet which is the modern English representative of the old mawls and malls. The surviving mawl-men of England are engaged in the game of croquet, mallet in hand; it is a long-drawn test of eye, hand, temper and patience that they undergo through the long summer day on a lawn that is a joy to look at as well as to tread. The old mawl suggests now the swashing blow: the mallet is for a suave follow-through shot or the precise passage of the all too narrow hoop.

METHODOLOGY

THIS looks like a modern horror but it has the authority of Coleridge. Properly used by him it means the science of method, the comparison of ways and means, even a philosophy of these things. But nowadays we love to tack the imposing -ology on to all manner of things, talking of a man's ideology when all we mean is his ideas. So was methodology employed as a pompous term for method by the American delegate to an International Conference on Cotton. He certainly had the lingo in full flood.

> We can provide not only substance but methodology for making policy decisions.

Another of his sentences ran

> The conference should identify and dissect the elements of the textile problem treating each one in its proper role of cause or effect, and make the result available to the agencies and personnel of statecraft.

Here is the polysyllabic periphrasis in its fullest flower. The final words, 'make the result available to the agencies and personnel of statecraft' presumably mean 'report to Governments'. What is the cause — or rather the aetiology — of such eloquence? Is a business or official man really thought to be a fool if he insists in using one short word where seven long ones can be put on parade? Shakespeare did not observe that there was methodology in Hamlet's madness.

MIM-FOLK

I LIKE mim to describe the pursers of lips, the too demure of speech and of behaviour. In a Scots poem 'Said the Spaewife' (fortune-teller) Dorothy Paulin has employed it vigorously.

> Said the auld spaewife to me –
> 'Never be humble!
> Lads'll tak' the rough o' your tongue
> An' never grumble;
> But the thing nae man can bide,
> An' he be human,
> Is that mim-moothed snivellin' fule,
> A fushionless woman.'

Fushionless is insipid, feeble.

Another of the poets quoted in Douglas Young's anthology of *Scottish Verse 1851-1951*, the Rev. Dr. Walter Chalmers Smith, used it effectively in his tributary verses to Miss Penelope Leith.

> Last heiress she of many a rood,
> Where Ugie winds through Buchan braes –
> A treeless land, where beeves are good,
> And men have quaint old-fashioned ways.

Of Miss Leith he noted,

> The quaint old Doric still she used,
> And it came kindly from her tongue;
> And oft the 'mim-folk' she abused,
> Who mincing English said or sung:
> She took her claret, nothing loth,
> Her snuff that one small nostril curled;
> She might rap out a good round oath,
> But would not mince it for the world.

Since my own ancestry is of well-beeved Buchan in Aberdeenshire I am naturally attracted by this portrait of the gay Miss Leith, for whom history ended with Prince Charlie and all Whigs were damned, although that part of Scotland was not greatly drawn by the Jacobite call. According to her poet, she broke all the decencies of a Victorian Sunday in Buchan by cosily playing whist while the Whigs were 'psalm-snivelling in the wind and rain' – the mim-folk!

Mrs. Gaskell in *Sylvie's Lovers* mentions a complaint that 'Wenches are brought up so mim nowadays: i' my time they'd 'a thought na' such great harm of a kiss.'

MINIBITION

I READ in an official brochure that their Twenty-first Anniversary Conference and Minibition was held by the Purchasing Officers Association amid the agreeable surroundings of Harrogate. Presumably a Minibition is a Minor Exhibition or a display suffering from modesty about its size. (Thus a Minor Exhibitioner of a University might bring himself up-to-date by calling himself a Minibitor.) On the Conference side of the Minibitionist activities was a discussion led by the 'Anglo-American Productivity Council's Production Control Team'. Why so lengthy? This is sadly out of tune with Minibiting. Could not this group be suitably reduced to Prococo? Their precise subject was 'Practice and Trends in American Procurement'. Procurement has a sinister sound, but it has become unimpeachably respectable. Does this title mean anything more than American Buying Methods?

Are there, I wonder, any Majibitions or Maxibitions? I cannot discover that our great-grandfathers spoke of the Crystal Palace Maxibition. The Purchasing Officers should annex this word, if word-patents are available outside the range of branded goods: otherwise the Psychologists, if they too, in frantic pursuit of brevity, become manipulators of the verbal telescope, will be using Maxibition for Major Inhibition and Minibition for some less infuriating frustration. Since trade is now so much inhibited by controls, the

Purchasers might like to have their minibition both ways. I am sure that the word minimal was much heard in the speeches of Prococo. To lecture on the minimal impediments to the most efficient procurement by Purchasing Officers is much finer Conference English than to talk about the least hindrance to good buying.

The gathering had its social round and joys of sight-seeing. 'For the Ladies. A Coach Tour via Blubberhouses Moor to Bolton Abbey, returning via Ilkley Moor where coffee will be served.' Doubtless full-sized coaches were needed for those Bolton-bound, but had the volunteers been few they could have travelled in a minibus. In the nineteenth century this charming term was actually applied to the tiny version of an omnibus and even, playfully, to a cab. It would be a nice sign of Lilliputian modesty to say that you are just off by minibus to see a minibition.

MITHER AND DISJASKIT

CHESHIRE appears to be a richly inventive as well as a stubbornly retentive county in its matters of vocabulary. Or is it simply that it produces more word-lovers who want their favourites to live on and kindly let me know it? Doubtless other shires keep that fine slab of sticky sound, slutch, for mud and share with England's Deeside mither (to rhyme with neither) for pester. One who was told in his boyhood to stop mithering people explains it as a telescoped version of muddle, rile and bother. I suppose that it is a cousin of 'moider' which is still used with much the same sense over a fairly large area. Earlier I mentioned doddled as a word for bothered. 'Botheration' has a plentiful outfit of descriptive terms.

There is, for instance, disjaskit. This has dictionary status with the limiting remark that it is Scottish. But it is a Somerset man who writes to me on its behalf. *O.E.D.* limits its use to broken and decayed things. It is doubtless a corruption of the Latin disjectus, most familiar in the neuter plural, 'disjecta membra poetae'. But disjaskit is now quite as much used of disturbed people and their states of mind as of scattered and untidy things. It means put out, distraught, depressed, mithered, and moidered, and is too good to lose.

MOFF

I HAVE commented before on the simple country words for effeminacy, i.e. lass-lad. A new one to me is moff, which is an abbreviation of hermaphrodite. We all know that the dual purpose of the Royal Marine, soldier and sailor too, earned him the Kipling beauty, 'giddy harumfroditie', which is far more imposing than moff. A moff, apparently, is a term for a dual-purpose dray which can be turned into a cart of safer conveyance by adding boards on each side. So the men of the modern road have their scholarship. The child of Hermes and Aphrodite wanders far afield from Greece.

MUFFATEE

SOMETIMES a muffler, sometimes a woollen cuff slipped on in winter; more often it was the latter and certainly so to C. S. Calverley since he uses it in the plural for a single wearer.

> till a ladylike sneeze
> Or a portly papa's more elaborate wheeze
> Make Miss Tabitha seize on her brown muffatees.

This occurs in *Under the Trees*, a demonstration of virtuosity in rhyming. There are forty-three consecutive lines all ending with the same rhyme. True, some proper names are included, but Calverley hardly ever used the same sound twice with a different spelling, as he surely might have done, i.e. frieze and freeze, quays and keys, tease and Tees.

He included Ratafias – pronounced Ratafees.

Then Tommy eats up the three last Ratafias
And pretty Louise wraps her *robe de cerise* –

It is notable that the ingenious poet managed to include some internal rhyming, as in the Miss Tabitha line and in that about Louise. Including them, there are fifty-three consecutive rhymes on the ending in ees, eese, ease, eeze, etc.

I do not know why ratafias became ratafees in pronunciation. But I do know why Tommy gobbled them. Ratafia was originally a liqueur flavoured with crushed stones of fruit or nuts, especially of almonds. Then, as a sweet, crunchy, almond-flavoured biscuit the ratafia is, or was, delicious. Does it survive? I do not notice it in the catalogues of the Higher Biscuitry. Ratafias may nearly rhyme with austerities, but the two do not harmonize.

MUMRUFFIN

I LIKE this cheerily bedraggled word for a long-tailed tit, the most architectural of our small birds and one who plans his nest as though intending a cathedral. I note that it has attracted other informal names. One of these, according to a *Times* Christmas Quiz, is Feather-poke. I prefer mumruffin, with its suggestion of a quietly roguish little fellow. While on this topic, why, I would ask, was a goldfinch called a chelandry? That nimble-minded young pretender, Thomas Chatterton, while fabricating his medievalisms, gave this example of English 'as wroten bie the gode priest, Thomas Rowleie, 1464'.

In Virginè the sultry sun 'gan sheen,
  And hot upon the meads did cast his ray;
The apple ruddied from its paly green,
  And the lush pear did bend the leafy spray;
  And pied chelandry sang the livelong day;
'Twas now the pride, the manhood of the year,
And eke the ground was dight in its most deft aumere.

Aumere is interpreted as robe and the pied chelandry as the goldfinch. I think that Master Rowleie might have admitted a mumruffin to his boskage. As a specimen of Olde Fudge Chatterton's lines may be said to take Ye Guerdon.

MUSE-RID

EXCELLENT for a hyperaesthetical young man. But Pope must have had not the ebullient fantastic but the skinny pedant in mind when he wrote:

> No meagre, muse-rid mope, adust and thin,
> In a dun night-gown of his own loose skin;
> But such a bulk as no twelve bards could raise,
> Twelve starveling bards of these degenerate days.

I suppose the days have, by convention, always been degenerate and poets starveling. Can a man be muse-rid and monstrous? Since I regard G. K. Chesterton as having been, on many occasions, a truly great poet, the answer is 'Yes'. But 'a meagre mope, adust and thin' he certainly was not; nor was his skin a dun night-gown. Mope as a noun might be kept in use; now we talk rather of 'a misery'.

OVICAPITATE

IN one of my previous volumes I mentioned the term Muse-brows, used by Elizabeth Barrett Browning to describe the fore-heads of the Artistic Nine, and proposed that it might be a suitably descriptive title for a certain type of poet, the servant of the Nine. Has not the British Broadcasting Corporation's team of intellectuals, worthy to be called Muse-brows, been working with valiant application to supply its Third Programme? Whether or no we accept Muse-brow, we have to admit, surely, that Highbrow and Low-brow have been worked to death – with Midbrow insufficiently accepted. Now comes the Egg-head, alluded to by the more learned as the Ovicapitate.

The Egg-head has a smooth, oval head, like one of the elliptical billiard-balls mentioned by W. S. Gilbert's Mikado. This vessel is packed with mental meat which may or may not be in decay. The weakness of the word lies in the possession by so many intellectuals of plentiful and undisciplined tresses: they are as shag-haired as any villain in Shakespeare. Still, there are, too, the nude and glittering domes, wherein great thoughts abound.

Do Egg-heads resent their new name? I quote this from the London *Bookseller*:

> My friend Mr. Miles W. Standish of Forest Gate, a self-confessed egg-head, offers a slogan or rallying-cry for others of that oppressed minority. Though not quite up to Mr. Standish's usual high standard I pass it on freely to more militant campaigners: 'Eggheads of the World Unite: You have nothing to lose but your Yokes.'

But what chance would an Egg-head have in any scuffle? The heavy thatch of the Muse-brow would have its protective power, but the brittle shell of the Ovicapitate is an argument in his case for avoidance of all battle.

We can derive from antiquity some tribute to the value of long-headedness. Is the Ovicapitate very different from the Dolichocephalic (long-headed) Man in the antiquarian's list of types? The Dolichos, we know, preceded the Brachycephalics (short-headed), but they were beaten by the latter's possession of better weapons, using iron against bronze and both against stone. But if the long-heads managed to create the long barrows, the stone avenues, and the great stone circle of Avebury they were considerable planners, weight-lifters, and architects in stone, and so are fit to rank even with the more exalted Ovicapitates.

PAGAN

IT has evidently an attractive and romantic sound, since in one of the most popular of picture-strip narratives, that of Rip Kirby, spectacled tower of protection for the righteous weak, the much harassed heroine has Pagan for a Christian name. Would the creators of these daily openers of our sticky morning eyes ever take Christina for a heroine? I fear not. The pagans win. Dear Pagan Lee, may Kirby keep you ever free from robbery, rapine and demise. I do not doubt that he will. But for months – or is it years? – it has been a close-run thing.

Pagans began life as villagers, the Latin 'pagus' naming them. But, since villages, in the pre-radio world, got the news last, pagans were still 'suckled in a creed outworn' when the townsmen were becoming converts to Christianity. So pagan became a title for all recusants of the new faith. However urban a Jew might be, he was none the less pagan to the medieval Christian. But no amount of the contempt injected into the word by Christian intolerance could rob it of beauty. 'Most beautiful Pagan, most sweet Jew.' Jessica was not insulted by the name now deemed worthy of Rip Kirby's adorable Miss Lee.

'The name of those fabulous animals (pagan, I regret to say), who used to sing in the water, has quite escaped me.' Thus Mr. Pecksniff spoke of the Sirens. ('Not swans, very like swans too. Nor oysters, but by no means unlike oysters.') It was typical of Mr. Pecksniff that he should regret paganism. But to his credit must be put his correct use of the word fabulous, which has now become an adjective of continual and maddening use by writers in search of a picturesque term for anything remarkable or even just large, e.g. 'Fabulous crowds swarmed on the beach at Blackpool.'

Pagan, like fabulous, has been abominably abused in our own time. Its proper meaning, since the old villager notion is long dead, is non-Christian and a non-Christian may put his faith in creeds which are certainly not contemptible and in philosophies which are noble and austere. But pagan has become confused with the base, the sensual, and the degraded, for which error there is no excuse save ignorance, if excuse that be. So we find pagan given the same pejorative sense as heathen and used merely to denote savagery, which is indeed hard on the Stoics and those of their descendants who live by a strict and selfless moral code without acceptance of the Christian dogmas. Infidel is another sufferer from religious persecution. There is no reason why a non-believer in Christianity, who has been brought up in a different tradition or has worked his passage philosophically, should be confused with the savage addicts of Mumbo-Jumbo. Properly used, the word pagan should have no moral implications. It refers to belief, not behaviour.

PEJORATIVE

THIS alternative to depreciatory has become a vogue-word with the *litterati*. It might be an adjective meaning anything that makes worse just as meliorative (or ameliorative) is applied to anything which makes better. Political measures or persons could be pejorative in that sense because they create nuisances; but more commonly nowadays the word is applied to a state of mind or a type of judgment, in which low valuations are to be expected.

Most activities have aspects which can be described in a pejorative way. There is actually a pejorative suffix, -aster. A criticaster is a poor sort of critic, pretentious but of small authority. A poetaster is also a pretender, assuming an inspiration which he lacks. That suffix is not always to be found when contempt is expressed: a philanderer, not a philaster, is a lover considered in a pejorative way. One would expect some sort of -aster to be found in the scientific field, but the fraudulent claimer of such knowledge is called a sciolist. This last has a sharp sting about it, and the professor who dismisses his rivals in some field of scholarship as mere sciolists has inflicted a prettily pejorative slap on the pale cheek of another man's learning. Then there are the sophists, who in Greece were not at first despised. But pejoration set in and these one-time instructors were regarded as the peddlars of philosophy, the mountebanks of logic and of metaphysics. So now they rank with the sciolists.

P-AMINOBENZOYL-M-PHENYLENEDIAMINE

ARITHMETIC to the rescue! I read in an article in *The Observer* that

> the basic organic chemical known as p-Aminobenzoyl-m-phenylenediamine, and its friend m-Aminobenzoyl-p-phenylenediamine, are now referred to more easily by their numbers 220-360 and 220-370 in the United States Commodity Classification.

This is good news for students, whose Higher Authorities seem bent on achieving a record by creating the world's longest word. The classicist had done his best with the honorificabilitudinitatibus mentioned in *Love's Labour's Lost* as one of the tit-bits of Holofernes and Armado in their feast of words. The Modern Side wins by three letters and doubtless it has bigger and better compounds on the way.

PEPPER

TO pepper a man is now to sprinkle him with pellets, either with leaden pellets in the shooting field or with verbal ones in the world of criticism. To say that a book had been peppered would hardly suggest that it had been flattered. Yet it would have meant that in the eighteenth century. It was written of David Garrick, perhaps unfairly,

> Of praise a mere glutton, he swallowed what came
> And the puff of a dunce, he mistook it for fame.
> Till his relish grown callous, almost to disease.
> Who peppered the highest was surest to please.

To Falstaff peppering was of the modern kind. 'I have led my ragamuffins where they are peppered: there's not three of my hundred and fifty left alive and they are for the town's end, to beg during life.' From Mercutio, 'I am peppered, I warrant, for this world' was declaration of the end, inflicted by steel and not by lead. What is remarkable is that, while the eighteenth century used peppering of the kind word, we have gone back to the Elizabethan idea of the lethal action.

PERPILOCUTION

SINCE I have included in a previous volume the verb Nigroglobulate for to blackball, I feel it only fair to accept Perpilocution for talking through one's hat. But questions may be raised, since pilus in Latin is a hair while pilos in Greek is a hat. Does not perpilocution more correctly mean talking through one's wig or thatch and might not a wearied and tetchy judge request the wigged counsel of a British Court to perpilocute no longer, since I take it that talking through your wig implies much the same as talking through your hat? I wonder why talking through one's hat came to mean talking nonsense, for the words in question must have passed through the brain, which all words do not. This reminds me of Lord Morley's reply to the man who told him that all good things come from the heart. 'No doubt, but they should go round by the head.' I suppose that, in full, the word should be perpilolocution.

PERSONABLE

I NOTE an advertisement in the Personal Column of *The Times* which announces the willingness or even eagerness of a Personable Young Woman to become a confidential secretary (the adjective would in the past have been unnecessary since confidential was exactly what the word secretary implied – or used to imply). The lady is ready to be an aid in many tasks and troubles. Why, I wonder, does she choose the adjective personable? It refers, I suppose, more to the figure than to the spirit. It is the quality of the physical person and not of the personality that is usually proclaimed by the word. But it is a very queer word: why the termination in -able?

But then so much is odd in this matter of personality. To be a Person was something of rank – or a term of abuse and contempt. To be a Personage was higher still. But the word could be ironically used. To be called a Personality is also a compliment to one's character and its achievement. But to deal in personalities is to be cheaply and meanly abusive. So there could be a Personable Personage with undeniable Personality: this would include praise of look, acknowledgment of status, and admiration of mental qualities, tact and charm.

There is a fascination about the adjective personable. It has an old look and sound, but seems to be quite young. I suppose that those who use it imply something rather more than prettiness. The Personable Young Woman is, to my imagining, of good stature and commandingly handsome: no employer, however much attracted, would think of her as his Baby, Honey or Sugar.

PIDDLE

THIS is not only 'to make water, now vulgar', in dictionary definition, but to be fussy with one's food, to pick at it and peck at it and trifle with it.

> Give order that twelve pigs be roasted yellow,
> Nine geese, and some three larks for piddling meat,
> And twenty woodcocks.

So did a Jacobean, Simon Tanner, who has the title-part in Middleton's *The Mayor of Queenborough*, order a dinner. Simon also used the verb in its vulgar sense. 'Like beast as I was I pissed out the fire last night and never dreamed of the king's coming.'

Pope, a century later, also trifled thus with his food.

> Content on little I can piddle here
> On broccoli and mutton all the year.

But the vulgar sense has now so far overcome the proper one that the children of today are unlikely to be rebuked for piddling with their dinner.

PLOOK

THIS Scottish word for a nasty pimple or boil seems to say everything of a physical blemish and of its capacity to create a sense of shame. The impostumes known to the Elizabethans sound more dignified, and also more formidable. Smollett's Doctor L., who came to Bath 'to ply for custom' and talked with such profundity as to madden Mr. Bramble (no difficult achievement) submitted a wart on his nose to the not very tender handling of young Mr. Melford. Caustic was applied later but the wart 'spread in such a manner as to produce a considerable inflammation, attended with an enormous swelling: so that, when he next appeared, his whole face was overshadowed by this tremendous nozzle'. Nozzle or plook? Neither sounds as impressive, and perhaps neither may be as painful, as a carbuncle or impostume; but they have a mean squalor of their own.

POST-MORTEMIZATION

IT is a peculiar fact that, while fewer and fewer learn Latin, our language seems increasingly to be latinized. An excuse is now so constantly called an alibi that usage has rendered even those who know what alibi does mean accustomed to, and tolerant of, the mistake. Post-mortem similarly creeps in as the imposing name for any kind of inquiry into error. A game of Bridge must be preceded, if peace and happiness are to be sustained, by the laying down of harmonious conditions – 'No post-mortems'. A correspondent has sent me from Australia an observation made at a Military College by the Minister for the Army when he was addressing cadets. 'I mention this,' said the statesman, 'in no spirit of post-mortemization.' To post-mortemize is not a verb which the purists will approve; but there it is, and doubtless it will be widely adopted.

Post-mortemization is the business of the coroner. Why was he so named? Originally he was the officer of a district charged with maintaining therein the private property of the Crown. It was a curious development of functions which turned the royal agent into one chiefly known as the conductor of inquiries concerning dead bodies of all classes and conditions. The alteration was an early one, for 'the crowner' to Shakespeare meant the officer responsible for 'sitting on' the victims of what we now tactfully call a 'fatality', since that implies no guilt and pre-judges nothing. 'Go thou and seek the crowner,' said Olivia to Feste when Sir Toby was oppressed with early lethargy and the repetitive nature of pickled herrings. 'Let him sit on my coz, for he's in the third degree drunk; he's drowned.' In *Twelfth Night* there is some bandying of long and learned words, especially on the lips of the clown. To pocket a tip with Feste is to impeticos a gratillity. But he never suggested to his lady that he should post-mortemize her crapulous uncle.

PRESSURIZE

HERE is an addition to the Horrors List. Does signatured mean any more than signed? Does pressurize mean any more than press? Some man of science will, I am sure, inform me that it does in the laboratory. But it certainly does not in the world of politics, where pompous asses think that their rhetoric sounds more important if they add a couple of syllables to a simple word. An Australian

Price Commissioner not long ago announced with pride, 'We will not be stampeded or pressurized.' That makes a bad impressurization on me. Must history books be brought up to date and given full honours of officialese? When they tell of naval recruiting in Nelson's time I can foresee some statement such as this: 'The Pressurization Gangs rapidly implemented the combat personnel almost to redundancy despite the fact that availability of manpower had been described as far from optimum.'

RAINBOW

FOR simple description rainbow is hard to beat. You may say that only the substance and the shape are there, not the colour. But we cannot have everything in two syllables and seven letters. The word is dear to me because of Ralph Hodgson's unforgettable

God loves an idle rainbow
No less than labouring seas.

These lines do not, if you insist on being logical, put forward an arguable proposition. But an entire philosophy is hinted at, and one of the functions of poetry is to give a hint in words that haunt. There are couplets and lyrics which come bubbling out of one's subconscious, superbly irrelevant to time and place. Hodgson's idle rainbow and labouring seas have come to my eyes and lips in the depths and din of a crowded London tube train. Alliteration, as usual, helps to implant them in a firm and affectionate recollection. The four 'l's are laced with the 'b's and 's's in the kind of pattern that is usually victorious. Many of the greatest lyrics in our language have a vague content: they touch the mind a little and the feelings much: it is the pattern of the sound, usually quite a simple alliterative device, that gives them permanence. 'All the breath and the bloom of the year in the bag of one bee' may overdo it; the author of 'Where the bee sucks' knew better. Witness the play of 'l's in 'In the cowslip's bell I lie'.

Ralph Hodgson had a marked fancy for the bow in the sky.

> Is still thy mind for wrens and little springs
> And ferns and sudden stoats and popping mice,
> And all the myriad noisy rainbow wings
> That make the wood not less than Paradise?

This is from 'The Last Blackbird', a poem that gave its name to an early volume, a poem that has also been given far more urgency by the ever-growing power of man to blast Nature with machines and wither her with chemicals. Hodgson, despairing of man's handiwork, called for a new Flood, an ocean-bath, 'to wash my world, a deeper, wider sea'.

The Scottish poets, who insist on the broad Scots, are emphatic in calling a rainbow a water-gaw. Scottish patriotism fails me at this point. Rainbow is ten times the better word and was good enough for Sir Walter Scott.

> What skilful limner e'er would choose
> To paint the rainbow's varying hues,
> Unless to mortal it were given
> To dip his brush in dyes of heaven?

No, I do not respond to water-gaw. When Dullness comes, in Alexander Pope's opinion,

> Before her Fancy's gilded clouds decay
> And all its varying rainbows die away.

But water-gaws might remain to welcome her.

RAMEKIN

IN a *Times* Fourth Leader called 'Under the Hammer' there was some pleasant scrutiny of 'The Valuable Contents of the Mansion'. One Sale Catalogue put together 'Peafowl, Antique Man Traps, Garden Statuary'. Obviously, as they say, here was 'something to go for'. In our years of incessant and violent burglary the Antique Man Trap, though the setting of it is, I suppose, illegal, must have its appeal for those who put a rough security before a nice legality. The leader-writer, enjoying his catalogue, adds, 'Its style, though sedate, is rich. Cassones and torchères, ottomans and fauteuils, tazze and tureens and ramekins, garnitures and purdoniums – we feel ourselves transported to a world of rather exotic opulence.'

I have previously noted the word purdonium as a stately piece of Auctioneers' English for a coal-box; ottomans, fauteuils and tureens are familiar articles of luxury or use. (The tureen, though it sounds lordly, has a humble origin, being 'terrine', the earthenware pot.) Torchères we can guess at. They might be brandished by the new-fangled torch-singers who afflict our nightly revels. (A Torch Singer is a terrible creature, at least as defined by Wilfred Granville in his *Dictionary of Theatrical Terms*; he describes her as a sentimental songstress 'who shines her torch in the face of a male in the audience', thus embarrassing him and amusing others.) A Tazza is a shallow ornamental bowl supported on a pedestal. Cassones elude me. Are they the same as caissons or chests? Garniture has, I suppose, some particular significance for Auctioneers, but, in any case, it is a nice word for appurtenances, the dressing of a dish or of a man. Dryden's phrase 'Men of feather and garniture' employs it prettily.

Now for ramekin. *O.E.D.* interpets it as 'a small quantity of cheese with bread-crumbs, eggs, etc., usually baked and served in a special mould'. But the 'cheese, bread-crumbs, eggs, etc.' would be in a curious state of decomposition if kept for the sale which eventually follows the decay of the Gentleman's man-trapped Estate or of the Nobleman's peafowl-strident Seat. So, the ramekin must here signify the special mould itself and not the mouldy fungus growing upon its surface. However, in this Penicillin Age we have been well instructed never to be harsh to a fungus or to brush off a mould as though it were a pestilence. Far otherwise. The decaying ramekin may yet bring us something of astonishing power to heal and save.

The list of articles for sale is an International Gathering, and reminds us that the English milord was a magpie when he made his Grand Tour and would pick up all manner of curious furnishings and garniture. An excellent place in which to study the rich relics of such collection is Charlecote, near Stratford-upon-Avon, once the mansion of that Sir Thomas Lucy whose deer-park Shakespeare may or may not have feloniously invaded. (There is no contemporary evidence to back the legend.) The Lucy and later the Fairfax-Lucy family have been collectors as well as travellers and their home, now in the possession of the National Trust and open to the public, reveals this change of taste and widely scattered purchases down the centuries. One might even find cassones and torchères there – or a ramekin.

RASHER

RASHER has a comfortable, sizzling suggestion. Disraeli, in *Coningsby*, mentioned 'the still hissing bacon and the eggs that looked like tufts of primroses'. The rasher frizzles deep in the British consciousness of simple satisfaction. But it has its mystery. Why is it limited to fried or grilled bacon and ham? Beef and mutton, whether hot or cold, are cut in slices. So are cold bacon and ham. But rasher was once bestowed upon pork, presumably cold since it was eaten with 'green sallard' by the eighteenth-century diarist Thomas Turner of East Hoathley. But he spelt rashers as ratios. Is the rasher a corruption of ratio?

A ratio is 'the relation between two similar magnitudes in respect of quantity, determined by the number of times one contains the other'. The word ration, so dismally familiar to the British for nearly a decade and a half, must be a development of the ratio. The relation between the magnitude of a man and the magnitude of one ounce of cheese or one egg a week has been a matter of long and melancholy experience. Presumably the idea of ratio as reason comes into it. Rations are rational sharing in times of scarcity as well as mathematical proportions. But did the successful rasher really spring from the same arid ratio and the meagre ration? If so, the child is fatter than the sire, another case of 'puppy-fat'.

REGRATE

ONE of my favourite country towns is Appleby, which many now whirl past – not through, to their loss and to Appleby's gain in quietude – as they scuttle on their motoring way to and from Scotland. Round it curls the river Eden in the green vale between the smooth surge of the highest Pennines and the sharper summits of the Cumbrian peaks. Appleby sounds like a Devonshire name, but it merits that mellowness, since it is a sheltered spot though neighbour to the loftiest and bleakest relics of England's wilderness. Appleby and Eden together are a jocund contrast, as well as gentle company, for the severities, scenic and nominal, of Yad Moss and High Cup Nick just above them. Though tiny and little larger than a big village, Appleby has authority; it is a County Town; and hence these notes on regrate.

I was reminded of the word by reading the reprint of some of the old Appleby records. We think of ourselves nowadays as much beset by controls, with Enforcement Officers – spies and snoopers, if you prefer – nosing into our business. But controls are as old as the Middle Ages and so are the snoopers too. The ale-taster was a ubiquitous guardian of brewing standards (Shakespeare's father held the office in Stratford) and the retailer was under continual survey. To forestall and regrate was among the latter's vices. To regrate was to buy and hold for a higher price in time of scarcity and at Appleby the regraters were busy during a potato shortage in 1799. So John Taylor of Crosby Ravensworth was 'amerced ninepence' for regrating in this market and the verdict was doubtless popular, since 'the poor were being deprived of their chief support'. How did the English poor manage before Sir Walter Raleigh helped them out with his imported batata? There were fewer of those poor, it is true, but one would have thought that the daily and native bread would still have been the staple in 1799.

Bread, too, was carefully watched and weighed and graded by authority. There were four qualities in Appleby in the eighteenth century. Wheat Loaf was controlled at nine ounces to the penny. Fine Teamsit, Martin, or Boult Bread at fourteen, Rye Bread at fifteen, and the 'Coarse Bread commonly called Barnard Castle' at sixteen. Weights were inspected once a month. Why was Barnard Castle so named and rated so low? Was there a jest on its stony quality? Was it Westmoreland's way of dismissing Durham and contrasting the fat vale of Eden with the leaner lands of Tees? I can find no explanation of Teamsit, second in rank to the gentry's Wheat Loaf, but bolt or boult is an old name for a sieve so the Teamsit, Martin, or Boult was in some sort refined.

Another nice aspect of Appleby's regimen was its largesse to passers-by. 'Traveller that was robed' cost the town a shilling in 1704. (The gift of a winding-sheet to a corpse cost the citizens 10d.) Does 'robed' imply compensation in money, with a mis-spelling of robbed, or was the wanderer supplied with a coat? Two years later a 'decayed gentleman Traveller' was granted a shilling. Decayed is a word that has descended in meaning and is now applied mainly to things and persons so far gone as to be in actual dissolution or at least 'daddocky'. The older and gentler meaning of impoverished has almost vanished. Sir Walter Scott used it so. Oswald of Devorgoil, central figure of his unsuccessful play, *The Doom of Devorgoil*, revived with more piety than glory in the Pitlochry Summer Theatre in 1952, was described by the author as 'A Decayed Scottish Baron'.

Appleby, incidentally, gave us the phrase 'as soon as you could say Jack Robinson'. For Robinson was the local Member of Parliament and apparently suspect of an itching palm and sticky fingers. When Burke was discussing corruption in the House, another member challenged him to give names and he replied with the neat evasion, 'I could tell you, as soon as I could say Jack Robinson'. Robinson was not caught out and may have been wholly innocent.

Possibly he knew a thing or two about regrating. At any rate he has this curious immortality.

REQUISITE

'THERE are two poyntes requisite unto salvacion.' Thus Sir Thomas More. But, when I saw in a shop a placard announcing Religious Requisites, I realized that there were more than two. The phrase Religious Requisites gave me a slight shock, because I had seen this imposing word Requisite applied so widely elsewhere in the service of a general commerce. This is Trade English and does not penetrate the home. No wife would say to her husband, when setting out on a visit, 'Have you packed your toilet requisites?' Yet if the man went out to buy some razor blades, he would probably find Toilet Requisites written large above the counter where the blades are kept. Our English stores abound in Requisites.

The story-tellers prefer to call them necessaries. Their heroes, especially detectives called out on active service, hurriedly throw a few necessaries into a bag. It is an old and Shakespearean usage. Both Hamlet and Othello had the word necessaries given to their light luggage. Requisites in Shakespeare refer to desirable characteristics. 'The knave is handsome, young, and hath all those requisites in him that folly and green minds look after', said Iago of Cassio before going off to get Othello's necessaries from the harbour. Shakespearean requisites were not on sale: they were aspects of Sex Appeal.

The women's fashion-notes make constant reference to Accessories, a word otherwise associated with crime. Accessories are a particular kind of requisite, being required to set off, by their colour and quality, the main garment to the best advantage. Handbags appear to be Accessory Number One, but gloves and shoes seem also to be on the Accessory List. I have never heard a man refer to his necktie as an Accessory, but this kind of thing may happen in the catalogues of the Higher Haberdashery.

Trade has added to the table of Requisites two other classifications, the Novelties and the Specialties. (Both these are covered, I suppose, by the comprehensive title of Fancy Goods.) The former are usually in the toy-and-trinket class; they are gift-goods and gew-gaws. The latter term is vague and crops up wherever the maker of a catalogue has lacked an obvious descriptive word for a species of goods for sale. With Specialty he plays safe. Both Novelties and Specialties are, as a rule, Unnecessaries, being for amusement and bedizenment, not solid use.

Requisites, on the other hand, are urgently required. The stubble demands its razor blade and the corn its cure (Foot-joy Requisite). It is sometimes argued now that brisk use of a toothbrush (see Dental Requisites), once deemed essential to a gentleman's clean living, really does more harm than good by wedging foreign bodies, ripe for decay, in between the teeth instead of scraping them out. In that case, our hope is in the toothpick, preferably used in private. Whichever way you have it, the brush and the pick are among the 'few necessaries' that await a tossing into gentleman's bags; they have the dignity of Toilet Requisites.

That dignity was much enhanced in my view after I had seen devotional books and articles also wearing the same label. The toothbrush and the Bible are certainly not Novelties, Specialties or Fancy Goods. They are the props and companions of the nation – or at least of the nation's better elements. They are Requisites.

RUMPUS

A GOOD rowdy word that has had some two hundred years of life. It appears to have a technical meaning in the vocabulary of transatlantic house agents, since in the American *Saturday Review* I found an answer to those seeking a home in Peacham, Vermont. They could have a five-bedroomed house, completely furnished and equipped with a Rumpus Barn for thirteen thousand five hundred dollars. I take it that a Rumpus Barn is a place where the children can knock hell out of everything, themselves included. Or is it for the Barn Dance, Square Dancing and other High Jinks of adults – or both? Whatever it be, I like the sound of it and also its purpose of segregation. A barn for the Rumpustious and a parlour for the peaceful.

In the same column of announcements I read 'Nostalgic sea-country inn! Personably yours.' Few adjectives have been harder worked in recent times than nostalgic, which ought to mean consumed by sickness for home (not the past). To apply it to a place and that a strange one is indeed twisting the neck of the poor word. What can 'Personably Yours' mean? Is the inn personable in the sense of handsome or is there some confusion with the idea of personality in a house?

I am not attracted by the news that a 'Secluded house in the country yearns for loving winter occupant while waiting suitable buyer.' This emotional establishment is owned by a writer who prefers another writer's company. 'You pay fuel and utilities... perhaps nominal rent.' When I pay rent I prefer to know exactly what it is, even if it be a home that is as full of yearning as any Barrieish 'Island that Longs to be Visited'. The prospect of two writers sharing accommodation hardly suggests tranquillity to me. If artists get together, a Rumpus Barn is indispensable.

When an American hotel advertises 'continental cuisine' does it refer to its own or some other continent? It is understandable that the English, perched on the fringe of Europe, should mean European when they advertise continental cuisine; but since there are so many ranges of European diet and styles of European cookery, the claim is meaningless. The American country hotels advertising in *The Saturday Review* include in their attractions meals luscious and meals lucullan, while one small voice, most likeable, only promises 'good food'. As for the etceteras, is one attracted by 'Horses, Country Auctions' or by 'Sports, Friendly Informality'? The latter has a frightening sound, especially as there is no mention of a Rumpus Barn in which to isolate the informally sportive.

SALLY-MY-HANDSOME

ONE of the pleasing habits of the countryside is to dawdle over the names of flowers and even to draw them out. Long classical names are not necessarily abbreviated: they can be affectionately or amusingly altered into English sounds and even into English sentences. Cornwall appears to be happily addicted to this habit. Consider the word Mesembryanthemum. There is no connection with anything embryonic. Mesembria is the Greek for mid-day and the rest of the word is the Greek for flower. The flower so named is like the English Inns: it opens towards mid-day. But what a mouthful for an English countryman! So, in the Duchy, it becomes Sally-my-handsome, a name to adorn any 'floral tribute' or lover's posy. The friend who gave me this one adds that Somerset has turned the Biting Stonecrop into Welcome-your-husband-whether-he-come-drunk-or-nay. Here is a complete alteration of meaning and suggestion. For what could sound less welcoming and less warm and cosy than a Biting Stonecrop, which should be the emblem of the shrew? And what more bland, benign and charitable than the pardoning recipient of the male errant described in the much longer name?

SHOG

'LET the world shogg.' This I found in a collection of *Scottish Proverbs, Explained and made intelligible to the English Reader* by James Kelly, M.A. (1726). Kelly's explanation of this cosmic permit to shogg is 'Spoken by those who have a Mind to do as they have resolv'd, be the Issue what will'. The general sense is therefore parallel to that of 'Who wull to Coupar, maun to Coupar.' Obstinacy will out and no shogging of the world – i.e. shaking or rolling of the globe – will stop it.

Shog, with one 'g', was used by Shakespeare in the sense of leg-shaking or jogging along. He has it twice only and both times it is used by the same character in the same play, Nym in *Henry V*, and followed with the suffix 'off'. Perhaps he heard it in the street while he was working on this play, and then forgot it. One would expect so expressive a version of our buzz off to appear often in the comedies, if it appeared in one.

Slang terms for quit are always numerous in any language. In my boyhood we bunked or did a bunk. When did skedaddle, described as an American military term for unmilitary behaviour (1882), become established here? One descriptive word for flight is a re-import. I discovered 'beat it' in Ben Jonson and suppose it must have crossed the ocean and returned again. P. G. Wodehouse's characters are apt to shimmer out of the room, but that is hardly a skedaddle. 'Jeeves shimmered out and came back with a telegram.' Nothing so vulgar as shogging for Jeeves. The fashion of today has moved on from scram to what I think must be scarper: at least that is the noise that I hear made in plays and films about crooks, 'wide boys', and others who, like Shakespeare's Nym, have occasion to do some hasty shogging-off. Then there are the people who 'beetle away' when they vanish or vamoose: this last is a century-old American word which is sufficiently well regarded by *O.E.D.* to be given its place – and that next door to vamp. The latter has obviously failed to hold her prey when the man can shimmer out, scarper, shog off and vamoose.

SIBLING

OUR psychologists prefer, as a rule, long words of classical origin. They like, for example, to call lonely brooding involutional melancholia. 'Schizophrenia was coined by Bleuler in 1911 . . . it superseded entirely dementia praecox.' But in the Penguin book on *Psychiatry To-Day*, by David Stafford-Clark, from which I quote that sentence, I also find the use of a very old and simple word, sibling. This term, says the author, 'is a convenient one for describing children of the same parents whether they are brothers or sisters'. It is strange to find psychiatry drawing on Old England rather than on Ancient Athens, by way of Central Europe, for its vocabulary.

Sib is an Anglo-Saxon word for kin or akin. It lingers in gossip, which was originally god-sip, the baptismal sponsor. Why godfathers and godmothers should have been particularly associated with garrulity and so have bestowed their old font-side name on the vice of chattering about their neighbours is not plain.

SKULL-DUGGERY

IN one of Damon Runyon's short stories called 'Tight Shoes' there is mention of a racing gentleman who, afflicted with vanity, would pretend that his size in footwear was a small one. At his shoe-shop the usual assistant tactfully served him with a much larger shoe assuring him that it was the smaller size. Unfortunately the racing man, off to the track, one day encountered a new assistant who was not going to play down to human vanity in order to get a sale. Skull-duggery, it is written, was not for him. So the race-goer, being laced into inadequate leather, suffered severely, his pains being not at all mitigated by the fact that he backed losers all day.

Skull-duggery is familiar to the Scots in another and presumably earlier form, sculduddery, signifying for them obscenity either in action or in speech. But the word seems both to have crossed the Atlantic and taken on a new life. It is spelled differently and it has a different meaning, being limited in its reference to financial crookedness and having no connection with libidinous conduct or loose talk. Nobody knows the origin of the Scottish word sculduddery; nor is it possible to explain its curious alteration into skull-duggery. The brain has something to do with fraudulent practices, but the skull is usually the symbol of death, not of dishonesty.

SQUIGGLE

THE squ's suit slanting movements. We have squint, with the Shakespearean squinny, and squirm. The dictionary says that to squiggle is to 'writhe about', another form of squirming. I associate it with handwriting, and especially with the illegible signatures of the Squiggle family.

What is maddening in the conduct of these Squiggles is that they are not, as a rule, bad writers in general. They will send you a quite legible letter and then end with an indecipherable mess where the name should be. Here indeed is a 'writhing about'. It is as though a wasp had fallen into the ink and then, maddened, had squiggled over the paper.

Why does Squiggle squiggle in this way? Is it an overwhelming modesty which makes him feel that he is so trifling a creature that it really cannot matter whether his name be read or not? Or is it an overwhelming vanity which makes him feel that the world must recognize his mark? There are those who sign, Napoleonically, with a single letter. That suffices. In the same way Squiggle may believe that his inky sprawl is enough. The world should know it and be suitably impressed.

Often these letters need an answer and then one has to pore and ponder, look through the page to see how Squiggle makes his letters when he is not just squiggling, and so waste much time and trouble. Some writers compose cryptograms throughout; the medical profession includes many such, if their prescriptions be taken as evidence. Chemists, I suppose, know in advance much of what is being ordered; if not, they must have taken courses in deciphering as part of the apothecary's training.

There are sound-squiggles too. Specialists in this are the boys who 'page' names in clubs and hotels. They wander about making vague and plaintive imprecations, as though calling upon a Mr. Myah-Myah, always Mr. Myah-Myah. It is not surprising that this squiggle-scream rarely evokes any response from the chattering or sleeping figures to whom it is addressed. There is also the Squiggle

Introductory, uttered by the hostess who presents one as Mr. Mum-Mum to another Mr. Mum-Mum and leaves both parties completely ignorant as to whom they are meeting.

We have all sinned as Squigglers in some form or degree. My correspondents on verbal matters often take infinite trouble – with everything but their signatures. I am deeply grateful for their information and for their corrections of my errors. I do my best, with my secretary's aid, to interpret the queer splotch that is sometimes the signature. A grateful reply is needed. Can the Squigglers blame me if I write on the envelope, over the address,

A. Blank Squiggle, Esq.,

and leave it at that?

TRAMPOLINE

THE word comes from the circus where a trampoline act originally meant a turn on stilts. For some reason it was extended to the large, springy bed on which somersaulters leap with astonishing results in levitation. This kind of trampoline looks a fascinating toy; even the most senile and arthritic of codgers must feel that he could enjoy a leap and a toss on such a sweetly elastic foundation, which receives the returning human missile so cosily. Can midget trampolines be bought for the nursery or the playroom? Dangerous, perhaps, if overworked, but undoubtedly popular.

Trampoline as an adjective and bearing the old meaning of stilted might be transferred to literary criticism. Those wishing to dismiss a pretentious and woodenly phrased style without too much offence could dismiss its owner as one of the loftiest trampolinists of his day. The trouble is that the circus trampoline has so oddly shifted from a feat of elevated stiffness to a bouncing machine producing the utmost agility and vivacity. Having just read Miss Tallulah Bankhead's book of memoirs I should call her the queen trampolinist (in the social sense) of autobiography. Her Anglo-American argot, describing the kind of life she leads when she is down to her last magnum, is charmingly acrobatic.

TRASH

TRASH is the 'top and lop' of the copse and spinney, the bits and pieces lying about when the thinners and pruners have done their work, the raw material of bavin. The use of it for material rubbish or human worthlessness was a natural transition. There is a verb to trash, meaning to cut away. Prospero used it of statecraft.

> Being once perfected how to grant suits,
> How to deny them, who t'advance, and who
> To trash for over-topping.

But to trash is also a picturesque verb for to walk or run with exertion and fatigue. Trashing about town nicely sums up the weariness of getting about among crowds on a dismal, drenching day. I came across it during some investigation of the minor Jacobean dramatists. 'I still trashed and trotted for other men's causes', said one of the characters in Thomas Middleton's *A Trick to Catch the Old One*. In the same speech there is the strange word fooliaminy. The lawyer Dampit called his clients, not in their hearing, 'the fooliaminy and coxcombry of the country'. For such trash he had to go trashing about the courts. The -aminy termination was dear to Master Dampit. He also spoke of bawdreaminy.

TROLLOPE OR SLAMMERKIN

DURING a visit to a provincial church in 1756 Cowper records the spectacle of 'several negligees, with furbelowed aprons, which had long disputed the prize of superiority; but these were most woefully eclipsed by a burgess's daughter, just come from London, who appeared in a Trollope or Slammerkin, with treble ruffles to the cuffs, pinked and gimped, and the side of the petticoat drawn up in festoons'.

Here dress-making dances its verbal minuet. Let us trace the steps backward. I have always liked the look of the word festoons, the garlands of a festival. Since we live in a period much addicted to Festivals and can hardly arrange a couple of concerts without somebody calling the affair by the high Festival name, we should be free with our festoons. Festoons of petticoat are a nice conceit. A festoon was also, in architecture, a carved ornament. 'Flora and Boys in *alto relievo* supporting festoons', to quote Horace Walpole, was part of the dignity of a mansion. Nowadays it suggests something in a more grandiose pantomime or spectacular revue – possibly on ice; but let Flora be: I cannot read of festoons without delight.

Gimping, too, excites a pleasant curiosity. 'Silk, worsted, or cotton twist with a cord or wire running through it.' (The gimping and goring of the costumier's art unreasonably suggest the bumping and boring of jockeys.) Pinking is a fencer's word. The duellist pinked a body with a thrust: the dress-maker ornaments by perforating or punching little holes. Pinking the raw edge of silk was scalloping a pattern on it. And so to Trollopes.

The Trollop was a sluttish woman before she was a rakish one. Carelessness of attire was later connected with laxity of conduct. Shakespeare, though he never used the word, had the arch-trollop in the Audrey of his Arden, who, denying sluttishness, thanked the gods that she was foul; to that Touchstone observed that, with foulness present, sluttishness would come hereafter. From the untidy trollop came the trollope or trollopee, a loose garment in which the trollops might trollop about – for the noun has its verb. Then the carelessly worn wrapper of the slut was elevated to be the negligee of the elegant. A lady could ask for her trollopee without loss of dignity. It was, as Cowper observed, Church-worthy and Sunday-go-to-meeting attire.

I do not know whence the family name of Trollope came; but we may reasonably imagine an ancestress who earned the title from supercilious neighbours. She need not have been an Audrey, but rather one who played up to Herrick's notion of the careless charmer.

> A sweet disorder in the dress
> Kindles in clothes a wantonness;
> A lawn about the shoulders thrown
> Into a fine distraction.

With a 'tempestuous petticoat' and 'ribbands to flow confusedly' he pictures the trollope-de-luxe who, a century later, would have donned a trollopee.

Slammerkin is, likewise, a word of double application. It means both the slatternly woman and the loose covering she may like to wear. (The favourite initial letters for untidiness are plainly indicated by sloppy, slouching, sluttish, and slatternly slammerkins. Idleness comes into the same alphabetic category with slothful, sluggish, slumping slummocks.) It is not known whether John Gay's Mrs. Slammekin of the *Beggar's Opera* gave a new name to the trollop and the trollopee or whether these derived their slammerkin title from the character in the piece, as Grundyism came from Mrs. Grundy who was another party of the play. She was mentioned in Thomas Morton's *Speed The Plough*, which is very rarely revived in these days.

It was a finely echoing boudoir in which milady could cry out for a slammerkin or trollopee.

TUNDISH

IT sounds like an adjective applicable to one of a violent nature and so given to striking blows and causing contusions. Winchester School kept this Latinity of tunding in its penal code. 'A contumacious and tundish fellow, a swashing, dam-you-ram-you knave' might swagger and bully in an old comedy. But tundish is, in fact, a noun of Shakespearean usage and some rustic employment still.

A Cheshire correspondent has told me of an old gardener who always spoke of a tin-funnel for filling lamps or other vessels as a tundish. It was the habit of Shakespeare's Lucio to give a rude twist to most of his terms and notions and so he played with a tundish in describing Claudio's offence. The salacious comedians have been at it since then. The old music-hall song which inquired, 'What's the use of an old tin-kettle if it hasn't got an old tin spout?' was given with a wink which Lucio would have comprehended.

Tundish reminds me of Standish, a tray for inkpot, pens, etc. Dorothy Osborne tells of an uncle who threw the standish at his man's head because 'he writt a letter for him where instead of sayeing (as his Master bid him) that he would have writ himself but that hee had the Goute in his hand, hee sayed that the Goute in his hand would not permit him to put pen to paper; the fellow thought hee had mended it mightily and that putting pen to paper was much better than plaine writeing.'

TWIXT

IT decorates, from time to time, the announcements of houses for sale. You know, if you study these matters, exactly what will follow the caption, Twixt Mummerset and Moors. It will be 'an impeccable period gem'; it will have a 'wealth of exposed beams' – and perhaps a less publicized wealth of dry rot. It will have a quaint, old God-wottery garden. In a world of snarling realism house agents are the incurable romantics; not for them such a commonplace word as between, not for them even the full two syllables of the Middle English betwixt. Twixt it must be. It is not that the space occupied by the extra two letters has to be saved, for there is room to call placed 'positioned'. Moreover, there are six lines to follow in which the words veritable suntrap are as likely to occur as the adjectives bijou and character – for character has become an epithet in this school of composition. Character cottages are commonly positioned twixt Downs and Sea, with views always guaranteed unbroken but not likely, since development marches on, to be unbreakable.

I await an urban and central arrival of this romanticism. Why not 'Twixt Soho and Seven Dials, convenient warehouse. Suit potato-dealer'? And might not a little grey home in the West lie twixt Acton and Ealing, or in the South, twixt Balham and Tooting – or, anywhere, twixt Tube and 'Bus.

Twixt reminds me of twee. This the *Oxford English Dictionary* dates back to 1905. 'For tweet, minced pronunciation of sweet.' So it is sweet, dainty, chic. Twee gems are usually bedizened versions of the gloomy little town-houses once rented for very small sums to those whom the Victorians called artisans and now sold for quite large sums to those who are passionate devotees of the quaint. They have tweely painted doors and windows. In the country they are thatched cottages turned into week-end resorts for the benefit of the neighbourhood's industrial towns. These latter usually have twee names like Land o' Nod or Cozicot. Outside them are toad-stool-shaped stone seats on which, no doubt, the fairies, leaving the bottom of the garden, sit o' nights. For it is a sure sign of twee English that the 'f' in the word of shall be dropped, as in 'Peg o' my Heart' and in other 'Love Will Find a Way' fictions for stage or book-shelf. The twee is found in sweetest flower round certain harbours in Cornwall, where the streets are so quaintly narrow as to be unpassable and the immigrants so twee of taste as to be unbearable.

UNDER-BELLY

WHEN Mr. Churchill spoke during the war of the 'soft under-belly of the Axis', the phrase was criticized, if I remember correctly, by that informed and incisive columnist, 'Janus' of the *Spectator*. The belly is under the body of a quadruped: it does not need to be called an under-belly. Yet the larger word has a Churchillian richness which it would be a pity to miss.

To our fathers the mere mention of belly would have been shocking. I owe to V. H. Collins and his excellent book on *The Choice of Words* a reminder that Cory's Eton Boating Song originally exhorted the oarsmen to 'Pull, pull together with your bellies between your knees'. Mid-Victorian manners insisted that this should be altered to the ridiculous 'with your backs between your knees', which is not only anatomically preposterous but deficient in scansion. Since then, adds Mr. Collins, 'bodies' has been substituted for backs.

An idiotic modesty surrounded mention of the human body and limbs, a modesty which compelled even Dickens continually to write of trousers as unmentionables or inexpressibles simply because they covered the legs. This was applied also to the belly, which remained Biblical, and abdomen, which remained medical. Every mention of the stomach, although it was more genteel than belly, was an occasion, with some people, for sniggering and blushing. Hence the coy jest of Sir James Barrie's title for his play, 'Little Mary', which inflicted that silly phrase for some years upon 'the tummy', itself another playful evasion. Now we are back among the under-bellies and belly-aches, with no punches – or might one say paunches? – pulled.

UNDERNEATH

SOMETIMES I look at a simple word which has been facing me since childhood and I am suddenly surprised by its tenderness or queerness and its power to move the feelings. Old, familiar syllables are made new in the mind and become stirring and musical. Under is a word employed a score of times every day and underneath comes to the lips or the pen almost as often. The popular music-hall song of Flanagan and Allen, 'Underneath the Arches', had in its title that common touch of poetry which is present in most nursery rhymes and old jingles of the countryside. It is the urban reply to 'Over the Hills and Far Away'. I found the beauty of the much-rubbed syllables in underneath lit up, not only while murmuring 'Underneath the Arches' but still more when a friend sent me the following lines with a request to know their author.

> Underneath the growing grass,
> Underneath the living flowers,
> Deeper than the sound of showers,
> There I shall not count the hours
> By the shadows as they pass.
>
> Youth and Health will be in vain
> Beauty counted of no worth.
> There a very little girth
> Will contain what once the earth
> Seemed too narrow to contain.

It has a sound of Emily Dickinson to me. In any case, it is a poignant and a haunting sound, as it were of the wind in the cypress tree. To its sad fascination the two initial 'underneaths' contribute much. After this, I resolve to keep an open eye and ear for other essentially beautiful words mumbled and forgotten in the scurry of things.

VERONAL

THIS is diethyl-malonyl-urea, a white crystalline substance used as a hypnotic. Veronal is a shorter and a sweeter name. What was its origin? The reasonable suggestion has been made to me by Lionel Hale that it was called after the drug, available in Verona, which Friar Laurence gave to Juliet, promising her 'a cold and drowsy humour' and 'the borrow'd likeness of shrunk death' with subsequent awakening, after two and forty hours, 'as from a pleasant sleep'. I can see no better reason for applying this melodious label to diethyl-malonyl-urea.

WAY-WISER

THERE were reproduced in *Country Life* not long ago two photographs of Perambulators or Way-wisers; one was on loan to the Dorchester Museum, the other is in the possession of the Salisbury Museum. The former is the larger and more handsome; it is also more distinguished in early ownership – or rather tenancy. It was pushed from Sherborne to Crewkerne by Dorothy Wordsworth, who had it as part of the equipment of a furnished house called Racedown. It must not be supposed that she was taking a baby for this strenuous walk. She was perambulating not only in the sense of walking, but of measuring the distance as well. She satisfied her curiosity while she took the air.

The way-wiser, to keep the good Saxon term for the classical Perambulator, was a single wheel with handle and with a recording clock attached. The latter was capable of marking distances. The instrument was certainly in use during the seventeenth century and is mentioned in Evelyn's *Diary*. Mr. Macnaghten, author of the *Country Life* article on way-wisers, believes that Christopher Saxton, who mapped every county in England and Wales about a century before that, must have had his perambulating machine. The specimen which was trundled along by Dorothy Wordsworth was made by Thomas Wright (1711-86), Instrument Maker to His Majesty. It is beautifully fashioned, as the photograph revealed, a charming piece of craftsmanship in metal and wood. The Salisbury way-wiser is simpler, but no less gracious.

One would naturally like to have the word way-wisdom for the practice of road-measurement. But the 'wise' part of way-wiser comes from the German 'weisen' to show. It is a weg-weiser, but most happily Anglicized. Perambulators remained way-wisers until mid-Victorian times, when the modern 'pram' arrived. Perambulator for stroller, not on wheels, has been retained by James Bone in his books of delighted and delightful topography, *The London Perambulator* and *The Edinburgh Perambulator*. I have also at times consulted with pleasure a more parochial but richly informative volume called *The Islington Perambulator* written in the eighteen-sixties. In addition to its general meaning of going for a stroll or dander Perambulation had a specialized significance, i.e. to walk round the boundaries of a town or district in order to define and affirm those limits. If there were any question of distance in dispute, the perambulators of this kind may have pushed a perambulator of the way-wising kind to solve their problems.

WISEACRE

THIS ought, one feels, to be a complimentary word, since the acre suggests some width of wisdom. But the wiseacre is not the man whose 'mind to him a kingdom is', not the seemingly spacious intellectual but a pretentious fellow, assuming a wisdom that he does not possess. He was originally a wise-sayer. But, just as the soothsayer began life as one who speaks sooth, i.e. the real truth, and then was degraded to mean a charlatan who, in prophecy, made a guess at the truth, so the wiseacre was also put down a peg or two and his sagacity degraded. This wise-sayer, instead of speaking wisdom as he did in his early days, became a pretender to profundity, the wiseacre of the plain, blunt man's contempt. Among my Fleet Street annals I remember a report that a newspaper tycoon, of great ability but little sensibility, broke the heart of a gifted member of his staff, a contributor of charming essays (rather too good for their surroundings) by calling his work, in public, 'wiseacre stuff'. It is possible to put a keenly cutting edge on to the disparaging syllables of wiseacre.

Wizard is another word of this kind which has lost distinction. The wizard, like the wiseacre, was once the truly wise, the sage unqualified. Milton gave highest honours to the wizards by calling the Magi so in his 'Ode on the Morning of Christ's Nativity'.

> See how from far, upon the eastern road,
> The star-led wizards haste with odours sweet.

Yet to Shakespeare, writing earlier, the wizard was already suspect.

Peace, doting wizard, peace. I am not mad

indicates that the wizard, Dr. Pinch in *The Comedy of Errors*, is a trifle mad himself. The wizard mentioned by the Duke of Clarence in *Richard III* is not a philosopher, but a wiseacre.

What did Milton mean when he applied wizardry to landscape?

Nor on the shaggy top of Mona high
Nor yet where Deva spreads her wizard streams.

Since the friend mourned in *Lycidas* was drowned in the Irish Channel and Mona is the Isle of Man, this Dee is the Welsh and Cheshire member of that company. The adjective wizard in this case seems purely a compliment, as glamorous has become. And so, in our own time, it has continued to be, since it was for long the slang word for marvellous or superb, passing from R.A.F. lingo to that of the school-boy.

WOMPO

THE house of Whitbread takes a praiseworthy interest in the traditions of its craft and of the inns in which the ale is sold. It records this lore in books of pleasant appearance, one of which, called 'In Other Words', deals with the vocabulary of brewing and of the dispensing of its wares. Towards the close of this little volume I note that Wompo is an East London term for beer. Wallop I have long known as a name for the mild ale which is lighter and less richly 'hopped' than 'bitter'. I was surprised to find that the Whitbread word-book makes no allusion to swipes, which *O.E.D.* describes as small, poor beer or beer in general. The sound of swipes has seemed to me to indicate a certain contempt and to imply a poor quality of brew. But evidently Hilaire Belloc did not think so. He went to the extreme of favourable opinion in his use of it. In his 'West Sussex Drinking Song', having praised the beer of Haslemere, Guildford, and Amberley he decided,

> But the swipes they take in at the Washington Inn
> Is the very best Beer I know.

In youth, while walking thereabouts, I made a special journey to the Washington Inn to put this grave matter to the test. I decided that Belloc had been generous in his allotment of what might now be called an Oscar, or at least a gong, to the tipple in question. But his dithyramb was composed long before I made my trip. So he may have been correct in his time.

Wompo is a more genial word than wallop or swipes, both of which suggest physical violence. Another kindly term on the list of beers is Granny, which means a mixture of old and mild, as grandmamma should be.

ZENONIAN

A ZENONIAN attitude to life may be obstinate in two ways. The first Zeno was a philosopher of Elea who, in the fifth century B.C. disproved, as he thought, the possibility of motion. While I am naturally inclined to condole with the sage on the state of his bowels, the Zenonian assertion deserves, in other respects, some sympathy in our time of universal fidgets and of speeds in movement that reach the supersonic. It is certainly a trifle hard to prove his case since the whole of one's existence seems to consist of shifting things, words on to paper, ideas into heads, men into uniforms, and tourists into countries, as well as food into bodies and bodies to and from their work and play. However, I have previously quoted James Bridie's admirable argument that man's especial genius lies in his capacity for repose. To that extent Bridie was a good Zenonian. 'Budge not' seemed common sense to him.

The other Zeno, 'the budge doctor of the Stoic fur', he who two hundred years after his namesake had thus disposed of motion, disposed, more or less, of pleasure, would have been no friend of the Scottish doctor, dramatist, and best of companions. But even the strictest of the Stoic tribe must admit the claims of kindness and gallantry. And Zeno did. It was not that he would try anything once, but that certain temptations called forth his sense of courtesy rather than proving his weakness. Montaigne has related that 'They report that Zeno never dealt with woman but once in all his life, which he did for civility, least he should over-obstinately seeme to contemne the sex'. The *vie amoureuse* of the earlier Zeno is not, I believe, known. He may, perhaps, in one of his major fits of negation, have denied the possibility of woman. For is she not volatile?

ZEPHYR

THE softness of the word suits the caress of the breeze. Pope understood that.

> The sound must seem an echo to the sense.
> Soft is the strain when zephyr gently blows,
> And the smooth stream in smoother numbers flows.

So our eighteenth-century poetry abounds in zephyrs. This was due not only to the classicism of the period: the zephyr soothed the ear: it was 'echo to the sense'. Charles Kingsley's muscular Christianity rejected this tranquil, south-westerly, murmuring air.

> Welcome, wild North-Easter!
> Shame it is to see
> Odes to every zephyr,
> Ne'er a verse to thee.

'You can 'ave Rome', as the weary Cockney traveller said after a long day of rubber-necking. In the same way the Kingsleyites can have their North-Easter. I am for the zephyr. As for the word, no poet of the modern fashion would be seen within a mile of it.

The zephyr, except in the clothier's world, has had its day. But it may return. Poetry has its ups and downs and before long we may once more be writing of passion's raptures in the breast and of zephyrs as Aurora's escorts, inviting Corinna to the capers of a May-Day.

ZEST

IF you have ever slipped on a piece of orange-peel you may well curse zest for the resulting sprain. It began life as orange or lemon-peel: since this was used for flavouring, zest became a word for piquancy and then for the gusto which relishes piquancy. Now, it serves for any kind of eagerness.

So let me end these books on the last letter and with a word of delight. 'Z' is a happy letter, as 'y' is so often a sad one. For though 'y' stands for youth it suggests to me the sadness of youth lost and not the glory of youth in being. It is the youth of which one thinks, in one's sear and yellow leaf, lamenting dead yesterdays and yearning for the years that were. Years can sound almost as melancholy as tears and are close to yearn in connotation as well as in the dictionary. But the 'z's are full of vigour and fascination! The zephyrs bless us and make us zealous for zestful relish of the spring and lead on to the zenith of the summer. (I am conveniently forgetting the Zenonians.) There is many an exquisite line that lives in beauty by the grief that is in its 'y's.

> That time of year thou may'st in me behold
> When yellow leaves, or none, or few do hang.

'That time of life' would not ring the bell so movingly nor would 'faded leaves' affect me like the yellow ones.

'Z' makes no such dirge. One of the Greek words for life was Zoe. And so I shall end these anthologies in a 'Zedful' manner and with zest.